157

UNDATIONS OF MODERN PSYCHOLOGY SERIES

hard S. Lazarus, *Editor*

THE PSYCHOLOGICAL DEVELOPMENT OF THE CHILD, Paul H. Mussen

TESTS AND MEASUREMENTS, Leona E. Tyler

MOTIVATION AND EMOTION, Edward J. Murray

PERSONALITY AND ADJUSTMENT, Richard S. Lazarus

CLINICAL PSYCHOLOGY, Julian B. Rotter

SENSORY PSYCHOLOGY, Conrad G. Mueller

PERCEPTION, Julian E. Hochberg

LEARNING, Sarnoff A. Mednick

LANGUAGE AND THOUGHT, John B. Carroll

SOCIAL PSYCHOLOGY, William W. Lambert and Wallace E. Lambert

PHYSIOLOGICAL PSYCHOLOGY, Philip Teitelbaum

EDUCATIONAL PSYCHOLOGY, Donald Ross Green

THE NATURE OF PSYCHOLOGICAL INQUIRY, Ray Hyman

ORGANIZATIONAL PSYCHOLOGY, Edgar H. Schein

E D G A R H . S C H E I N

Professor of Social Psychology, Organization Studies Group, Sloan School of Management, Massachusetts Institute of Technology; researcher and author on the psychology of attitude and value change, brainwashing, interpersonal dynamics, and management development; consultant on management and organizational improvement; Fellow of the National Training Laboratories.

Organizational Psychology

PRENTICE-HALL, INC., *Englewood Cliffs, New Jersey*

ORGANIZATIONAL PSYCHOLOGY, *Edgar H. Schein*

PRENTICE-HALL FOUNDATIONS
OF MODERN PSYCHOLOGY SERIES

Richard S. Lazarus, *Editor*

PRENTICE-HALL INTERNATIONAL, INC., *London*
PRENTICE-HALL OF AUSTRALIA, PTY., LTD., *Sydney*
PRENTICE-HALL OF CANADA, LTD., *Toronto*
PRENTICE-HALL OF INDIA PRIVATE LIMITED, *New Delhi*
PRENTICE-HALL OF JAPAN, INC., *Tokyo*

Designed by Harry Rinehart

C–64108(*p*), C–64109(*c*)

Foundations
of Modern Psychology
Series

The tremendous growth and vitality of psychology and its increasing fusion with the social and biological sciences demand a new approach to teaching at the introductory level. The basic course, geared as it usually is to a single text that tries to skim everything—that sacrifices depth for superficial breadth —is no longer adequate. Psychology has become too diverse for any one man, or a few men, to write about with complete authority. The alternative, a book that ignores many essential areas in order to present more comprehensively and effectively a particular aspect or view of psychology, is also insufficient. For in this solution, many key areas are simply not communicated to the student at all.

The Foundations of Modern Psychology is a new and different approach to the introductory course. The instructor is offered a series of short volumes, each a self-contained book on the special issues, methods, and content of a basic topic by a noted authority who is actively contributing to that particular field. And taken together, the volumes cover the full scope of psychological thought, research, and application.

The result is a series that offers the advantage of tremendous flexibility and scope. The teacher can choose the subjects he wants to emphasize and present them in the order he desires. And without necessarily sacrificing breadth, he can provide the student with a much fuller treatment of individual areas at the introductory level than is normally possible. If he does not have time to include all the volumes in his course, he can recommend the omitted ones as outside reading, thus covering the full range of psychological topics.

Psychologists are becoming increasingly aware of the importance of reaching the introductory student with high-quality, well-written, and stimulating material, material that highlights the continuing and exciting search for new knowledge. The Foundations of Modern Psychology Series is our attempt to place in the hands of instructors the best textbook tools for this purpose.

Preface

The field of organizational psychology is new and in flux. This fact creates for the writer of a textbook both a challenge and a problem. The *challenge* is to contribute to the ultimate shape of the field by providing certain points of view and certain focal concepts around which to organize thinking. The *problem* is to do justice to the massive history of the parent fields of industrial psychology, industrial sociology, and social psychology. Whether I have been able to meet the challenge will have to be judged by the reader and critic. The solution to the problem I can judge to some degree myself.

I have consciously and deliberately selected only certain concepts and reported only certain research studies to illustrate these concepts. No attempt has been made to give an overview of the many studies which have been done on behavior in various kinds of organizations. A list of selected books is provided at the end of the volume for the reader who wishes to pursue some of these areas further. I have also reluctantly left out a discussion of theory building and research methodology. In this field, there are unique problems of how to do valid research which, unfortunately, have only been alluded to in the text. Therefore, the student should not expect to find a final picture of the field from reading this book. Instead, I hope he will come away intrigued, puzzled, and stimulated. Organizations are part of our daily life. Whether the student pursues the study of organizational psychology or not, this text should open his eyes somewhat to the complex phenomena which are occurring around him at all times and of which he is wittingly or unwittingly a constant part.

I benefited greatly from the helpful comments and suggestions of my late colleague, Douglas McGregor, whose ideas have inevitably influenced me deeply. I would also like to thank Warren Bennis, Chris Argyris, Richard Lazarus, and the 1964–1965 class of Sloan Fellows who gave me the benefit of their reactions to an early draft. Mr. Ronald Nelson's editing often turned an incomprehensible sentence into sense and helped to organize the material. Finally, I am indebted to my wife, Mary, for providing a climate in which I could work productively, and to Mrs. Marian Pruslin for her excellent editorial assistance and typing.

Edgar H. Schein

Contents

THE FIELD OF ORGANIZATIONAL PSYCHOLOGY

Page 1

The Development of the Field.
The Plan of This Book.

1

PSYCHOLOGICAL PROBLEMS IN ORGANIZATIONS

Page 6

What Is an Organization?
Psychological Problems
in Formal Organizations. Recapitulation.

2

RECRUITMENT, SELECTION, TRAINING, AND ALLOCATION

Page 18

3

*Recruitment, Testing,
and Selection. Job Design and Human
Engineering. Training.*

ORGANIZATIONAL MAN AND THE PROCESS OF MANAGEMENT

Page 43

4

*Types of Organizational Relationships. Management's
Assumptions about People. Recapitulation:
Authority, the Psychological Contract, and the Process
of Management in Perspective.*

GROUP AND INTERGROUP RELATIONSHIPS

Page 66

5

*Definition of a Group. Types of Groups
in Organizations. Functions Fulfilled by Groups.
Variables Affecting the Integration in Groups
of Organizational Goals and Personal Needs. Intergroup Problems
in Organizations. The Problem of Integration in Perspective.*

Contents

THE ORGANIZATION AS A COMPLEX SYSTEM

Page 88

6

*The Organization in Relation
to Its Environment.
Toward a Redefinition of Organization.*

ORGANIZATIONAL EFFECTIVENESS

Page 96

7

*Maintaining Effectiveness
through an Adaptive-Coping Cycle.
Organizational Conditions
for Effective Coping. Conclusion.*

SELECTED READINGS

Page 107

INDEX

Page 109

Contents

xi

Organizational
Psychology

The Field of Organizational Psychology

An area of psychology typically develops around some questions that involve human beings. The questions may be primarily of concern to the practitioner such as teacher, parent, or manager who is trying to resolve some pressing problem; or they may reflect some area of interest which the scientist has developed. The field does not develop, however, until there are available conceptual models, theories, and research methods for gathering and analyzing relevant data. Thus when we have both a focus of interest and a way of studying it, we have the beginnings of a new "field."

1

The effective utilization of people in organized human effort to produce goods and services has always been a pressing problem. The pharaoh building a pyramid faced problems fundamentally similar to those faced by the corporation executive of today. Both must figure out (1) how to organize work and allocate it to workers; (2) how to recruit, train, and effectively manage the people available to do the work; (3) how to create work conditions and reward and punishment systems which would enable the workers to maintain high effectiveness and sufficient morale to remain effective over long periods of time; (4) how to adjust their organization to changing environmental conditions and technological innovations; and (5) how to cope with competition or harassment from other organizations or groups within their own organization. These and many other questions, which lie at the heart of any "organization," have been faced and resolved by politicians, managers, and bureaucrats throughout history.

Psychologists became interested in such organizational questions only as their theories and methods enabled them to think constructively about the questions and to test their thinking with empirical research. They started with questions which deal with the *assessment and selection of individual workers* and ignored those questions which involve the organization as a whole. Thus, the earliest successful efforts of industrial psychologists involved the testing of recruits in order to enable organizations such as the Army or a large industrial concern to improve their selection methods. Selection was made more scientific by *measuring* in individuals those characteristics which the organization required of its new members. The organization itself, however, was merely a source of information and of questions to be answered. It supplied the goals to be achieved; the psychologist worked to help fulfill them.

But with this more scientific and systematic approach, psychologists soon found themselves moving closer to organizational problems, in a growing attempt to put order into the process of *designing and organizing work itself*. Industrial psychologists found themselves working closely with engineers to analyze the basic characteristics of work in order to give each individual worker a job which maximized (1) his human capabilities and limits; (2) coordination and teamwork among employees, and (3) over-all efficiency. Thus, "time-and-motion" studies were carried out to determine how competent workers actually perform a given job; "job analyses" were carried out to standardize the work and to enable managers better to select and train workers; physical surroundings, noise levels, fatigue, monotony, and other accompaniments of work were studied to determine their effect on the quantity and quality of work. Still, however, the organization served only as the environment; it defined the ultimate products or services to be obtained and enlisted psychologists to help them study human performance with the aim of making it more effective.

As psychologists studied workers, it became clear to them that the *systems of rewards and punishments created by organizations* have a major impact on

The Field
of
Organizational
Psychology

2

the effectiveness of workers. Psychologists became increasingly interested in rewards such as pay and promotion and punishments such as reprimands as motivators and as conditioners of learning. The long tradition of studying human and animal learning made it possible to redefine and test within the organizational context many of the hypotheses which had been worked on in learning experiments. The kinds of incentive schemes used by management thus became still another major focus of industrial psychologists.

In delving into the motivations of workers, the psychologists also found that a worker's relationships to other workers make more of a difference than they had reckoned with. For example, how hard a man works may have as much or more to do with how hard his co-worker works as with how much money he will make or how hard his boss drives him. It became clear that *an organization has within it many groups which generate their own norms of what is right and proper behavior, and that such norms extend to the amount and type of work to be performed.* In looking at management more closely, psychologists also found groupings within a particular organization based on the managers' functions, ranks, or geographical locations. In some cases, groups, such as the sales department and the production department, compete with each other to the point where their own ultimate effectiveness and that of the organization as a whole is reduced.

It was in the study of worker motivation, incentive systems, personnel policies, and intergroup relations that the organization as a total system first began to come into focus. Psychologists recognized that for an individual member, whether worker or manager, an organization as a whole exists as a psychological entity to which he reacts. The quality and quantity of his work are related to his image of the organization as a whole, not just to the immediate characteristics of the work or his immediate monetary incentives. Furthermore, it was recognized that the individual does not stand alone in relation to the organization but is integrated into various groupings which themselves have patterns of cooperative, competitive, or indifferent relations to one another. In other words, the deeper psychologists delved into the behavior of individuals within organizations, the more they discovered that *the organization is a complex social system which must be studied as a total system if individual behavior within it is to be truly understood.* It was this discovery which created organizational psychology as a discipline in its own right.

Let me repeat this point because, in a sense, it is the keynote to this entire text. Organizational psychology as a field is intimately tied to the recognition that organizations are complex social systems, and that almost any questions one may raise about the determinants of human behavior within organizations have to be viewed from the perspective of the entire social system. The difference between the industrial psychologist of the 1920's, 1930's, and 1940's, and the organizational psychologist of today is thus twofold: (1) Traditional questions—such as those of recruitment, testing, selection, training, job analysis, incentives, work conditions, and so on—are treated by the organizational psychologist as being interrelated and intimately tied to the social system of the organization as a whole. (2) The organizational psychologist has begun to concern himself with a new series of questions which derive from the recognition of the system characteristics of organizations. These questions deal not so much with the behavior of individuals as with the behavior of groups, subsystems, and even the total organization in response to internal and external stimuli. The traditional industrial psychologist either would not have considered questions such as these or he could not have dealt with them scientifically because he lacked the necessary theoretical and research tools.

Two examples will highlight the difference between the traditional concerns and the "new" questions which organizational psychology is raising. First, given a rapidly changing technology which requires a great adaptive capacity on the part of organizations, how can an internal environment be created for the members of the organization which will enable them to grow in their own unique capacities? The underlying assumption is that unless such personal growth takes place, the organization will not be prepared to cope effectively with an unpredictably changing external environment. Second, how can organizations be designed to create optimum relationships between the various subgroups which tend to develop within them? For example, how can intergroup competition be converted to intergroup collaboration? The underlying assumption is that intergroup collaboration will be related both to over-all organizational effectiveness and to individual productivity and morale. Questions such as these recognize that the psychological forces operating on an individual are intimately bound up with what happens to the group or the total organization within which he operates.

Forces toward the Systems Point of View

In the above discussion, we have considered in very rough terms the development from individual-oriented industrial psychology to systems-oriented organizational psychology. Before concluding this introductory section, however, it would be well to mention some of the forces that stimulated and aided this development.

1. The penetration of sociological and anthropological conceptions into psychology and the growth of social psychology exposed psychologists to a whole range of new concepts and research methods. Although concepts like social role, status, social class, reference group, culture, and social system were developed outside of traditional psychology, they have become increasingly important in psychological analysis. New research methods—such as surveys by large-scale questionnaire or interview, the use of participant observation, and field experiments—have stimulated psychologists to go beyond introspection and laboratory experiments. It is these concepts and these methods which made it possible to tackle organizational problems, and which have shifted the focus of analysis away from the individual per se to the individual as a member of a group or to larger units like groups and organizations.

2. The development of new theories in the physical and biological sciences has made available different ways of thinking about psychological problems. Concepts of multiple causation based on a field of simultaneously acting forces have replaced mechanistic notions of simple cause-effect; concepts of mutual dependency and interaction, of feedback loops and self-regulating forces have made it possible to analyze complex systems and their relationship to the external environment. Such concepts have also made it possible to begin to develop theories within organizational psychology.

3. The rapid and tremendous changes in technology and organization that

have occurred within the last several decades have forced scientist and practitioner alike to recognize the interdependency of human and technological factors and the need to develop theories and concepts which can encompass such interdependencies. For example, we have seen the growth of man-machine systems within industry and military operations where it no longer makes scientific or practical sense to ask where the man leaves off and the computer or the machine begins.

4. Practitioners themselves have come to recognize the complex world in which they must operate and have been increasingly willing to have social scientists help with organizational problems. Thus, psychologists have become more involved in higher management decisions and have been brought into organizational positions from which they could more easily see the complexities of organizations. A corollary trend has been the increasing professionalization of management, with the result that managers are now technically more qualified than they were and, by the same token, more prepared to accept help from other professions. Thus, managers have become not only more aware of their needs for help from psychologists, but have also become more willing to use this help. This development, in turn, has made organizations more accessible to researchers.

5. Finally, psychologists themselves have become more skilled in dealing with problems of complex systems. They have, therefore, been able to help organizations to a greater degree; in return organizations have supported the efforts of those psychologists willing to tackle the more nebulous and difficult systems problems. Out of this increased interaction have come better theory and new research techniques.

THE PLAN OF THIS BOOK

The material covered in this book will reflect the general historical trend from an individual-oriented industrial psychology toward a group-and-systems-oriented organizational psychology. In Chapter 2, I will present an overview of the kinds of human problems that arise in and are generated by organizations; in doing this, I will attempt to provide a framework for thinking about organizations as social systems.

Chapter 3 will examine some of the traditional psychological problems associated with bringing people into an organization—recruitment, testing, selection, job design, and human engineering. In Chapter 4, our focus shifts to how an organization can productively utilize its human resources through an effective process of management. In Chapter 5, we will examine the integrative problems which arise because an organization is composed of many formal and informal groups, and we will discuss research bearing on intergroup cooperation and competition. In Chapter 6, our focus is the organization as a total system and the problems of survival, adaptation, growth, and change which it faces as it interacts with its environment and as it generates unforeseen forces within itself. Problems of "organizational health," total system effectiveness, and optimum integration of human and organizational needs will be discussed in Chapter 7.

The Field
of
Organizational
Psychology

5

Psychological Problems
in Organizations

In order to understand organizational psychology, we must first understand something about organizations. What are they? How are they to be conceptualized and thought about? What kinds of problems arise in them that involve psychologists?

It is surprisingly difficult to give a simple definition of an organization. All of us have spent our lives in various organizations—schools, clubs, community groups, companies and business concerns, government agencies, hospitals, political parties, and churches. Yet it is not easy to state just what constitutes *an organization*. Let us examine some of the ideas proposed by sociologists and political scientists as a context for this discussion.

6

2

First of all, it is important to recognize that the very idea of organization stems from the fact that the individual alone is unable to fulfill all of his needs and wishes. Because he lacks the ability, strength, time, or endurance, he finds he must rely on others for help in fulfilling his own needs. As several people coordinate their efforts, they find that they can do more than any of them alone could have done. The largest organization, society, makes it possible, through the coordination of the activities of many individuals, for all of its members to fulfill their needs. One basic idea underlying the concept of organization, then, is the idea of *coordination of effort* in the service of mutual help.

In order for coordination to be helpful, however, there must exist some goals or objectives to be achieved, and some agreement concerning the goals among the parties who are coordinating their effort. A second important idea underlying the concept of organization, then, is the idea of *achieving some common goals or purpose* through coordination of activities.

As we are all aware, organizations exist within organizations. Society is the largest unit, but within it there are economic, political, religious, and governmental organizations or institutions. Within each of these large units, we have many smaller units—individual business concerns, political parties, churches, and county seats. And within each of these units, we have smaller groupings of people which also, in a sense, are organizations—production and sales departments within a company, factions and cliques within a political party, a choir within a church, a police department within a county seat. According to some theories, these progressive differentiations arise out of the fundamental notion of *division of labor,* which is our third important underlying idea. Tied up with the concept of coordination and the rational achievement of mutually agreed upon goals is the idea that such goals can best be achieved if different people do different things in a coordinated fashion. Human societies have found that they can achieve their goals best if they divide up among different people the various functions which need to be fulfilled; hopefully the division is on the basis of different skills, but not necessarily so since people can be trained to do different things.

If each of the functions to be performed requires more than one person, the division of labor may be among organizations. Thus, an Army may decide that it is wise to have some men be fighters while others serve as supporters, bringing ammunition, food, and medicine to the fighters. But if the job of fighting and supporting are each big enough, they will be allocated to groups, and each group may then further divide up functions in order to achieve its objective. Fighters may divide into those who shoot rifles and those who man heavy guns. Suppliers may divide into a food-service unit, a clothing unit, and an ammunition unit. The total mission is divided into small units, creating the

---

[1] The ideas outlined in the next few pages are drawn from three sources: P.M. Blau and W.R. Scott. *Formal organizations.* San Francisco: Chandler Publishing Co., 1962; A. Etzioni (ed.). *Complex organizations.* New York: Holt, Rinehart & Winston, 1961, and J.G. March and H.A. Simon. *Organizations.* New York: Wiley, 1958.

possibility of a new organization to deal with each of these small units. The ultimate complexity of society thus rests in part on the belief, borne out by human experience, that our over-all goals can best be achieved by distributing very widely the subgoals and the labor needed to achieve them.

Our fourth and final concept is closely allied to the idea of division of labor and coordination—the need for a *hierarchy of authority*. It is obvious that coordination among many diverse individuals or organizations is not possible without some means of controlling, guiding, limiting, or managing the various units. The very idea of coordination implies that each unit submits to some kind of authority for the sake of achieving some common goal. If each unit pursues its own self-interest and disregards the activities of other units, coordination has, by definition, broken down. However, the idea of submitting to some kind of authority does not imply that the authority has to be external. Coordination can be achieved by voluntary self-disciplining activities such as those engaged in by two children operating a seesaw. The kind of authority implied by coordination thus can range from complete self-discipline to complete autocracy, but authority of some kind is an essential idea underlying organization.

As we all know from our daily experience, in most of the organizations in which we are involved, authority is usually embodied in a complex hierarchy of positions or ranks. Each position tends to have defined for it an area of responsibility (a division of the labor) and, theoretically, has the authority to insure that its part of the job will be done according to the plan as conceived by some higher authority. Coordination is thus implemented by the laying out by the highest authority of a kind of blueprint of who is responsible for what. This blueprint is constructed on rational criteria of how best to divide up the jobs and to coordinate them in order to achieve the over-all goal.

A Working Definition

We are now ready to put these ideas together into a working definition of what an organization is. This definition is similar to what the traditional organization theorist has started with. As we will see in later chapters, this definition will require modification as we bring the systems point of view to bear on organizational problems, but it will serve as a start.

An organization is the rational coordination of the activities of a number of people for the achievement of some common explicit purpose or goal, through division of labor and function, and through a hierarchy of authority and responsibility.

One important point in this definition which has not yet been discussed is that the object of coordination is *activities*, not people. As has been pointed out by many organization theorists, notably Chester Barnard, only some of the activities of any given person are relevant to the achievement of a particular goal. In fact, the same person can belong to many different organizations because in each one only some of his activities are relevant.[2] From the point of view of an organization, therefore, it is sufficient to spell out the activities or *roles* which must be fulfilled in order to achieve the goal. Some-

[2] C.I. Barnard. *The functions of the executive.* Cambridge, Mass.: Harvard Univ. Press, 1938.

one must fire a gun, someone must bring ammunition, someone must cook food. Which particular person fulfills the role may be quite irrelevant to the *concept* of organization, though it will clearly be relevant to how well the organization actually operates.

Because an organization is fundamentally a pattern of roles and a blueprint for their coordination, it exists independently of particular people and can survive in spite of 100 per cent turnover of membership. If the role expectations are recorded either in documents or in the memories of parents and teachers, the organization will continue from generation to generation with new members fulfilling the roles. In principle, the organization will only change when the blueprint itself is changed or when the roles are redefined by the top authorities or their occupants.

An organization, as we have defined it, is what the sociologists call a *formal* organization to distinguish it from two other types—*social* organization and *informal* organization. *Social organizations* are patterns of coordination that arise spontaneously or implicitly out of the interactions of people without involving rational coordination for the achievement of *explicit common* goals. A group of friends may coordinate their activities to a high degree and have common implicit goals such as "having a good time," but they are not a formal organization. If they choose to make their goals explicit and formally agree to certain patterns of coordination in order to *insure* having a good time, and if they establish some hierarchy to insure proper coordination, they would become a formal organization. In society, there are many patterns of social organization, such as the family, status systems, and communities. They are to be distinguished from formal organizations like business concerns, schools, hospitals, churches, unions, and prisons.

The description *informal organization* refers to those patterns of coordination that arise among the members of a formal organization which are not called for by the blueprint. The organizational blueprint requires the coordination of only certain activities. But for a variety of reasons, the human actors who fulfill organizational roles rarely can limit themselves merely to the performance of these activities. Two workers on an assembly line are only supposed to do their particular job; yet they may wish to talk to each other, to have lunch together, to share gripes about their job and boss, and in various other ways establish relationships above and beyond the formally required ones. Such relationships tend to arise in all formal organizations and can be thought of as the informal organization. As we will see, many of the important psychological problems of organizations arise from the complex interaction of the formal and informal organization.

PSYCHOLOGICAL PROBLEMS IN FORMAL ORGANIZATIONS

In our introductory chapter, we reviewed briefly the manner in which psychologists "discovered" and related themselves to organizations.[3] In the present section, I would like to present somewhat more systematically the kinds of psychological problems which arise in organizations.

[3] From here on, the word "organization" is used to refer to *formal* organization, since that will be our prime focus.

Recruitment, Selection, Training, and Allocation of Human Resources

Organizations are blueprints for human activities, but they do not begin to function until people have been recruited to fulfill the specified roles and to provide the specified activities. Therefore, the first and perhaps major psychological problem of any organization is how to recruit employees, how to select and train them, and how to allocate them to jobs for most effective role performance.

This broad problem can be broken down into two subproblems. First, a policy of recruitment, selection, training, and allocation designed to get the best performance out of people does not automatically insure that the individual needs which these people bring to the organization and expect to fulfill through organizational membership will in fact be met. Thus, one of the major dilemmas of organizational psychology arises because policies and practices which insure organizational effectiveness often may leave an individual's needs unsatisfied, or worse, may create problems above and beyond the ones the person brought with him. He may become alienated, insecure, and bitter if the organization fails to fulfill minimum needs for security, maintenance of self-esteem, and opportunities to grow and develop.

How, then, can organizational policies or social practices be developed which will permit the integration of human needs and organizational demands? Or, if these are fundamentally incompatible, psychologists must ask what other social institutions exist now or should in the future exist to ameliorate the problems created by individual-organization conflicts.

Second, the allocation and effective utilization of human resources can be pursued by two fundamentally different strategies which are based on entirely different assumptions.[4] One strategy, which has come to be identified with personnel psychology, puts its emphasis on selecting the man and fitting him to the job. The job is considered a constant while the human being is considered a variable. He can be selected and trained. From the total pool of human resources, one attempts to find those people who already fit organizational requirements or who can at least be trained to fit them. The other approach, identified with engineering psychology, puts its emphasis on redesigning the job and its physical environment to fit the limitations and capacities of the human being. The person is considered a constant while the job is considered a variable. Ideally, the job would be designed in such a way that *any* person could perform it. Both approaches can work and have worked in the past. *How then should one balance the testing-selection approach with the engineering and job-redesign approach in order to maximize the human potentials available to organizations?*

Utilizing Human Resources—Authority, Influence, and the Psychological Contract

If recruitment and allocation are the organization's first problem, then the motivation of people toward a high level of performance is its second and equally important prob-

[4] M. Haire. Psychological problems relevant to business and industry. *Psychol. Bull.*, 1959, 56, 169–94.

lem. Traditionally, this problem has been attacked by searching out and cataloging the motives and needs of workers, and relating these to the incentives and rewards offered by the organization. As studies have accumulated, it has become apparent that the problem is a complex one which can better be conceptualized in terms of a "psychological contract" entered into by both the individual and the organization.

The notion of a psychological contract implies that the individual has a variety of expectations of the organization and that the organization has a variety of expectations of him. These expectations not only cover how much work is to be performed for how much pay, but also involve the whole pattern of rights, privileges, and obligations between worker and organization. For example, the worker may expect the company not to fire him after he has worked there for a certain number of years and the company may expect that the worker will not run down the company's public image or give away company secrets to competitors. Expectations such as these are not written into any formal agreement between employee and organization, yet they operate powerfully as determinants of behavior.[5]

The psychological contract is implemented from the organization's point of view through the concept of authority, in that the decision to join an organization implies the commitment to accept the authority system of that organization. As I stated before, organizations coordinate their various functions through some kind of hierarchy of authority. Within defined areas a person must be willing to obey the dictates of some other person or some written directives or rules, and to curb his own inclinations, even if they are contrary to the dictates. Authority is not the same thing as pure power. Pure power implies that by the manipulation of rewards or the exercise of naked strength you can force someone else to do something against his will. Authority, by contrast, implies the willingness on the part of a "subordinate" to obey because he *consents*, he grants to the person in authority or to the law the right to dictate to him.

For such consent to be meaningful in a group or an organization, it must rest on a shared consensus concerning the basis of the legitimacy of the authority. That is, a law obtains our consent only if we agree that it is legitimate and right for us to be governed by it. An organization can give meaningful authority to a foreman only if the workers agree that the *system* by which people get to be foremen is one that they will support. It is agreement to the system that permits a worker to tolerate an occasional bad foreman and still take orders from him.

From the side of the worker, the psychological contract is implemented through his perception that he can *influence* the organization or his own immediate situation sufficiently to insure that he will not be taken advantage of. His sense of influencing the situation is partly the result of his agreement to the basis of consent, his acceptance of the system by which people have come to be in positions of authority; but it also rests on his sense of being able to affect the authority directly and to change his situation in the organ-

---

[5] This assertion is based on studies carried on by C. Argyris, reported in C. Argyris. *Understanding organizational behavior.* Homewood, Ill.: The Dorsey Press, 1960. Also by Levinson and his colleagues, reported in H. Levinson *et al. Men, management, and mental health.* Cambridge, Mass.: Harvard Univ. Press, 1962.

ization. The mode of influence—whether as a free agent or as a member of a union—is not so important as his fundamental belief that he has some power to influence if from his point of view the psychological contract is not being met. Thus, the organization enforces its view of the contract through authority; the employee enforces his view of the contract through upward influence.

The pattern of authority and influence that will result in any given situation depends in part on the *basis* of consent. The basis on which we accept the legitimacy of authority can vary from society to society and organization to organization. The sociologist Max Weber first pointed out, as the three major bases of legitimacy, tradition, rational-legal organization, and charisma.[6] These ideas are most easily illustrated if we think of whole societies and the political systems that underlie them.

Tradition as a basis of legitimacy implies that the governed grant authority to the ruler in the belief that his position has always been accepted. The clearest example is a monarchy which is supported ultimately by belief in the divine origin and rights of the ruling family and belief in the rightful inheritance by the oldest male son of the throne. Lower levels of authority are accepted to the extent that the king has delegated authority to them. What makes the whole system "right" is the set of beliefs or traditions surrounding the idea of monarchy. The organizational counterpart in our own society would be acceptance of the authority of an owner's son as senior manager, even if workers have questions about his actual ability as a manager. While we rarely see this kind of authority system in operation in our own society, it is still quite common in the political and business institutions of economically less developed countries.

Rational-legal principles as the basis of authority tend to be prevalent in our own society. They underlie the concept of a democracy and the idea of formal organization as outlined above. According to these ideas, power or authority should be assigned on the basis of rational criteria and in terms of procedures embodied in formal laws, contracts, and informal codes. Rational criteria imply that, in order to be given a position of authority, a person should have demonstrated the ability and motivation to fulfill the requirements of the position.

In the political sphere, these principles are expressed in the system of electing officials based on a rational assessment of their abilities, motivation, and prior service. In the organizational sphere, these principles are expressed in the idea of promotion based on merit (ability plus past performance) and in the notion that authority ultimately derives from a person's ability to do *something* better than those under him can do it, in short, his expertness. What the boss is expert at may be quite different from what the subordinate is expert at, as when a manager has under him ten chemists in a research lab. The acceptance by the chemists of their boss's authority rests on their perception that he is a better *manager* than they and that he has achieved his position by legitimate means.

Charisma as a basis for authority occurs in those instances where a very magnetic personality has been able to capture a following through belief in his

[6] M. Weber. *The theory of social and economic organization.* Talcott Parsons (ed.). Glencoe, Ill.: Free Press and Falcons Wing Press, 1947.

mystical, magical, divine, or simply extraordinary powers. Political and re-ligious movements often develop around charismatic leaders. They have their counterpart in organizational life in the instances where supervisors or top executives capture the consent of the members purely on the basis of their unique personal qualities. Thus, all of us have at times obeyed orders and followed leaders simply because we trusted them completely and accepted their word as dogma, even if they had neither expertness nor had earned their posi-tion by rational-legal means.

I have inserted this discussion of authority and its bases in order to under-line the point that an organization cannot function unless the members of it consent to the operating authority system, and that this consent hinges upon the upholding of the psychological contract between organization and member. If the organization fails to meet the expectations of the employee, and, at the same time, cannot *coerce* him to remain as a member, he will most likely leave. Thus, the problem of motivation and organizational incentives or re-wards is best thought of as a complex bargaining situation between organiza-tion and member, involving the decision of whether to join, the decision of how hard to work and how creative to be, feelings of loyalty and commitment, expectations of being taken care of and finding a sense of identity through one's organizational role, and a host of other decisions, feelings, and expecta-tions.[7]

To summarize, a second major psychological problem of organizations involves the nature and effects of the psychological contract between the organization and its members. Issues such as the nature of authority, the possibilities of influencing the system, the patterns of motivation and expecta-tions of employees and managers, the incentive systems generated by manage-ment, the management patterns that create loyalty and commitment as opposed to alienation and disaffection—all are part of this general problem.

Integration among the Parts
of the Organization

As I pointed out earlier,
division of labor is an essential aspect of organization. This division can result from specification of the various means by which a given end is to be accom-plished. Each of the means becomes the goal of the group of individuals to whom it has been assigned. This suborganization then generates its own means for accomplishing its goals and makes these the goals for further suborganiza-tions. Let us take again the example of the Army. In order to win a war (ultimate goal), the top authority decides it requires a certain amount of fire power, supplies, transportation, and so on (the various means to be used to accomplish the ultimate goal). As these means are made operational, they become the goals of the suborganizations which are made responsible for them. Thus, the infantry and artillery take as their goal the production of a certain amount of fire power; the transportation unit takes as its goal the provision of vehicles and the building of roads; the supply unit takes as its goal the

[7] The sociological bases of legitimacy have recently become the subject of research by a number of investigators who have attempted to determine the behavioral effects of different kinds of power. For a summary of this research see D. Cartwright (ed.). *Studies in social power*. Ann Arbor, Mich.: The Univ. of Michigan, 1959.

Psychological
Problems
in
Organizations

provision of ammunition, food, and other supplies. Each unit may decide that it can accomplish its goals best by further dividing the task in terms of various means to be used. Each of these means in turn becomes the end of some lower-order unit, and so on.

The total organization, then, can be seen as a system of ends-means chains wherein the means for a higher-level part of the organization become the ends for a lower-level part. The master blueprint of the organization often specifies only the first level of means to be employed, giving a certain amount of freedom to the next lower level to develop its own suborganization for optimum achievement of its portion of the total job. This situation creates the possibility, in fact, likelihood, that the different parts of the organization will begin to operate at cross-purposes with one another, overlap in function, or compete for scarce resources such as "good" employees or a certain "share of the budget."

In our Army example, the supply unit's decision to use their own trucks to carry ammunition, because they feel that a special kind of truck is needed, may conflict with the transportation unit's policy of supplying all transportation facilities. Or, worse, the roads built by transportation may not be suitable for the special vehicles built by some other unit. This example highlights overlapping or working at cross-purposes. Competition for scarce resources would be exemplified if transportation hoarded their best engineers even if some other unit needed their special talent, or if supply asked for a larger share of the total budget than they actually needed in order to insure that they could meet their goals. The larger the organization and the mission to be accomplished, the greater the potential lack of integration.

Thus, one of the major problems organizations face is the integration of their various parts to insure effective over-all performance.

But why is this a *psychological* problem? Why should it be considered in a text on organizational psychology rather than in one on organization theory per se? Why cannot integration be insured simply by a more careful over-all organizational plan which allocates functions in such a way that overlap and competition are eliminated?

The answers to these questions all involve the concept of *informal* organization. As we pointed out above, even though organizational roles demand only certain limited activities from each person, it is the whole person who comes to work. He brings with him many attitudes, feelings, and perceptions which are not anticipated by the organization and which do not clearly fit into its plan. As he works with others, he develops relationships to them, informal agreements, and patterns of coordination, all of which go beyond those specified formally by the organization. In fact, such informal procedures often are developed to cope with the problems which the formal procedures and regulations fail to cover. Many of the feelings, attitudes, and informal procedures reflect a growing loyalty to the subunit to which the person belongs. As he identifies with it, his self-esteem begins to be tied to its performance, and it becomes increasingly difficult for him to understand and empathize with the problems of other units and the organization as a whole. Increasingly, he may work for his own unit and become indifferent or hostile to the others. The formal organization often encourages this process by rewarding competition between groups and stimulating *esprit de corps*. The gains justify such competition but, at the same time, create intergroup coordination problems.

Many of the interunit difficulties which arise in the manner described and which reflect lack of integration are the product of *psychological* forces. Such forces operate in organizations toward the establishment of informal patterns which influence and alter the formal ones. Achieving greater integration, therefore, involves not only a rational redesign of the formal organization, but also psychological procedures which improve communication and mutual understanding among the subgroups within the organization, and thereby enable them to fulfill organizational goals more effectively.

Organizational Effectiveness—
Problems of Survival, Growth, and Capacity
To Adapt to and Manage Change

In this section we must consider the relationship of organizations to their environment. All organizations exist in an environment which consists of the culture and social structure of the society, of various other organizations that may stand in various relations to the organization under consideration, and various social organizations and groups of people who may be owners, managers, employees, customers, clients, or simply "the public at large."

In order to survive at all, an organization must fulfill some useful function. The common goals set by the architects of the organization must result in some product or service which is useful to the members of the organization or to other organizations or to the public at large. For example, Blau and Scott in their analysis of formal organizations use as the major basis for classification the criterion of who benefits from the existence of the organization.[8] They define four classes of organizations: (1) *mutual-benefit* associations, which benefit primarily the members of the organization, the rank and file (for instance, unions, clubs, political parties, religious sects, professional societies); (2) *business concerns,* which benefit primarily the owner-managers (such as industries, stores, banks, insurance companies); (3) *service organizations,* which benefit primarily their clients (for example, hospitals, schools, social work agencies); and (4) *commonweal organizations,* which benefit the public at large (government organizations such as the Bureau of Internal Revenue, Defense Department, police, fire department, research organizations, and so on).

The survival of each type of organization ultimately depends on its ability to continue to be of use to its prime beneficiary. The survival of an organization does not involve psychological problems different from the ones already cited. To survive, the organization must continue to perform its primary task —the recruitment, proper utilization, motivation, and integration of the people in it.

When we turn to the problem of organizational growth, we do uncover some new psychological problems, however. For example, organizational growth in a business concern may well involve the development of new products and new processes for making products which improve the competitive position of the company. New ideas for products and processes come from

8 P.M. Blau and W.R. Scott. *Formal organizations.* San Francisco: Chandler, 1962.

people. The organization, therefore, faces the problem of how to create an environment and a set of management policies which will not only get the primary task performed effectively but which will, in addition, stimulate creative thinking and innovation.

This is not a trivial problem because many of the procedures which organizations develop to maximize their day-to-day effectiveness lead to a psychological climate in which innovation and creativity may actually be punished. If such a climate has come into existence, how can an organization go about changing it without losing day-to-day effectiveness? Should innovation and creativity be expected of all members of the organization or should it become the assigned task of a few members who may be placed into a research and development group? If such a group is created, how should people be recruited into it, how should it be managed, and how should it relate to other parts of the organization? These and many other questions are psychological problems deriving from the issue of organizational growth.

Problems of growth relate closely to problems of adapting to and managing change. Organizations of today find themselves in a very dynamic environment. Technological change, which is proceeding at an incredible rate, creates constant problems of obsolescence. Social and political changes occurring throughout the world create a constant demand for new services and the expansion of presently existing ones. With the advent of computers and automation, the nature of organizations themselves is changing, bringing new needs for highly educated and trained managers far exceeding the present supply.

These environmental forces not only create a need for creative thinking on the part of members of organizations, but they also involve a more fundamental psychological problem. This problem can be conceptualized as follows: Much of the present technological and social change is unpredictable. We cannot accurately assess what will be the environment for organizations even a decade ahead. Therefore, if organizations are to adapt to such rapid and unpredictable change, they must develop flexibility and capacity to meet a variety of new problems. Such flexibility and capacity to deal with change ultimately rest with the human resources of the organization. If the managers and employees are themselves flexible, the organizational blueprint can be consciously and rationally altered in the face of changing external situations. If the people themselves are not flexible, then altering the blueprint will have no effect on the organization's operation anyway. The psychological problem for the organization becomes, therefore, *how to develop in its personnel the kind of flexibility and adaptibility that may well be needed for the organization to survive in the face of a changing environment.*

A closely related problem is that of the development of employees and management. One approach to raising the capacity of the organization to adapt to change is to develop to the utmost the capacities and skills of employees and managers. Part of the problem is to develop the particular management skills and capacities which the organization *knows* it will require in the future. But another part of the problem is to encourage the growth and development of the *unique* talents and capacities that the members of the organization possess, *even if those capacities and skills have no immediately foreseeable value to the organization.*

For example, the employee who ten years ago had a yen for pure mathematics and was encouraged by his company to educate himself in this area may find himself suddenly occupying a key role in evaluating the merits of conversion to automatic data-processing through electronic computers. If the organization is to make itself capable of adapting to and managing change, it may well have as one of its major psychological problems the encouragement of diversity of skills and the *psychological* growth of its employees. Such psychological growth not only may make management of change easier but may also ameliorate some of the other problems mentioned above, such as how to motivate employees, how to create commitment to the organization, and, most important, how to create a situation in which personal needs and organizational needs can both be satisfied.

RECAPITULATION

In this chapter, I have attempted to outline the major ideas underlying the concept of formal organization and the psychological problems which arise in organizations. These problems interact and overlap, but for purposes of rough classification, they can be divided into the following categories: (1) problems of recruiting, selecting, training, and allocating human resources; (2) problems deriving from the psychological contract between individual and organization, involving the nature of authority within the organization and the nature of the influence which the individual can exert on the organization; (3) problems of integrating the various units of a complex organization, which means to a large extent the improvement of communication and relations among the various informal organizations which arise in the formal structure; and (4) problems stemming from the needs of the organization to survive, grow, and develop the capacity to adapt to and manage change in a rapidly changing world.

In the next four chapters, we shall take each of these problem areas in turn and examine in greater detail the research and practical issues involved, review some of the major findings, and indicate what revisions in our theories about organizations seem to be required to take account of the research findings.

Recruitment, Selection, Training, and Allocation

In this chapter we will examine some of the specific procedures used in recruitment, selection, training, and allocation. We will examine some of the problems connected with these procedures, and attempt to show how these relate to other organizational problems.

One approach to the staffing of organizational roles is to recruit a pool of people who are likely to have the qualifications required and to select from among them those who will be most likely to perform the jobs well. It is often desirable to subject candidates to various tests or to observe them systematically in order to make it more likely that the candidate with the best qualifications is picked.

18

3

The process of recruiting candidates and of selecting from among them those likely to be of the greatest use to the organization existed long before the advent of scientific psychology. What psychology has been able to contribute to this process, however, is a higher average rate of success in selection; it has done so by applying scientific criteria to the whole selection process and by developing standard ways of observing candidates which permit systematic comparison and evaluation.

The steps required in order to improve the accuracy of selection are the following:

1. *Develop criteria*. The organizational roles or jobs to be filled must be adequately described to whoever is responsible for selection, and actual performance on the job must be in some way measurable.

2. *Determine predictor variables*. The candidate must be observed on some variables which are presumed to be good predictors of performance on the criteria.

3. *Obtain sufficient candidates to insure adequate variation on the predictor variables*. In order to determine whether the selection procedure is any improvement over pure chance or whatever method has previously been used, it is necessary to obtain candidates who rate both high and low on the predictor. If such variation is not obtained, it is difficult to establish a meaningful correlation between predictor and criterion.

4. *Hire an unselected group of candidates*. They should be hired without consideration of their scores on the predictor variable.

5. *Rate candidates on actual job performance*. These ratings must be obtained in order to correlate them with predictor-variable scores.

6. *Correlate scores or observations on the predictor variable with criterion performance in the unselected group of candidates*. This step is necessary in order to determine whether the predictor does in fact predict; if the correlation obtained is too low, another predictor has to be tried; if the correlation is acceptable, according to certain standards to be mentioned below, the next step can be implemented.

7. *Select from among further candidates only those who reach a certain score on the predictor variables*. Once a correlation has been established, it is possible to improve the accuracy of selection by using only candidates with scores similar to those of the unselected population who actually did well on the job. The actual cut-off score to be used depends on a number of factors to be mentioned later.

The improvement in selection which results from this type of procedure depends on a number of factors in the situation.

1. *The actual variation in job performance (the criterion) between best and worst workers*. If there is very little variation, a predictor has in fact nothing to predict. Hence, there is little point in going to the expense of developing one.

Recruitment,
Selection,
Training,
and Allocation

2. *The reliability of the criterion.* If, for any of a number of reasons, it is difficult to judge whose performance is better and whose performance is worse on a given job, or if the job is so complex that it is difficult to develop criteria in the first place, the criterion scores (ratings of performance) will be unreliable. If they are unreliable, it is difficult to establish a valid correlation between them and the predictor variables. It has been easy to develop tests and other predictors for clerical or manual work because a reliable criterion can be established. On the other hand, selecting managers, for example, has been much more difficult because of the problem of describing the managerial job and reliably judging relative performance.

3. *Success in locating predictor variables.* For many kinds of jobs it is easy to determine a likely predictor variable—for instance, manual dexterity for doing complex manual jobs, good vision for being a pilot, verbal fluency for writing advertising copy, and so on. For many kinds of jobs, however, the predictor may not be obviously relevant; hence, it may require great intuitive skill, much study of cases, and many unsuccessful experiments before a predictor can be located. For example, in the selection of managers, traits such as tolerance for ambiguity and emotional stability may be more important than specific managerial skills, yet they may not have been thought of as relevant when the managerial job was first analyzed.

Not only must a predictor variable be located, but it must be reliably measurable and it must enable one to discriminate among candidates. If all candidates get the same score, or if the scores vary from one testing to the next, it is impossible to establish a usable correlation between the predictor and the criterion.

4. *Enough candidates to be able to select and to insure variability in the predictor.* The sample of available candidates is largely out of the hands of the recruiter and selection specialist. One crucial point here is simply the number of jobs to be filled, what has been called the *selection ratio*. If the number of candidates is less than or equal to the number of jobs, it obviously does not pay to invest in an expensive selection procedure. Only as the number of candidates increases does a selection procedure begin to pay off. The greater the ratio, the greater the payoff, and, because of the sheer difficulty of deciding from among many candidates whom to hire, the greater the necessity for a selection procedure, as well. Closely related to the problem of the selection ratio is the problem of the *base rate*. The base rate can be defined as the percentage of *randomly* selected candidates who would be successful on the job. A high base rate can result either because all candidates happen to be highly skilled or because the job is one which could be done by virtually anyone. If for any reason all the candidates happen to have qualifications such that *any* of them could succeed at the job, it obviously makes little difference who is hired. Only if there is enough variability so that many candidates would be likely to do poorly at the job does it make sense to use a testing procedure.

5. *Enough time to determine the correlation between the predictor and the criterion.* One of the commonest mistakes in developing selection procedures is to skip the step of actually determining the correlation between predictor and criterion before using the scores on the predictor to select candidates. For example, a college desiring to improve the quality of its appli-

cants may decide to emphasize high school grades as a predictor. Before starting to screen applicants on this basis, it is essential that, for an unselected group, the correlation between high school grades and college performance be determined. This step is critical because it may turn out that there is no correlation, that the high school grades in fact do not predict. If this step is skipped and only students with high grades are admitted, it is difficult to obtain a usable correlation because of the reduced variability on the predictor variable. If the correlation in reality is low, the wrong students would be chosen for admission.

If an organization does not have time to test for such correlations with new samples of candidates, or if there is not enough turnover to permit the hiring of an unselected sample, predictor-variable scores can be obtained on present members of the organization and these scores can be correlated with their current and past performance ratings. The problem with the use of such existing samples is that they may already be highly selected in terms of the predictor variable, thus cutting down its variability, or their scores may be influenced by their actual experience on the job. In other words, for many tests, it is essential that the scores be obtained before the person has had specific experiences related to the test. If time is to be invested in developing a selection procedure, it is important to obtain actual correlations with the predictor before using it as a selection aid.

6. *A correlation high enough to improve the selection process.* Obviously the whole procedure hinges on success in predicting the criterion. No matter how much logical sense the predictor variable makes, or how much intuitive confidence the selector has in its use, if it fails to correlate with the criterion, its use will not improve the existing selection process. The correlation obtained is called the *validity* of the predictor: its capacity to predict what it is supposed to predict. How high this validity needs to be depends on the selection ratio, on the base rate, and on whether the organization is more concerned about obtaining successful performers (even if some unsuccessful ones appear also) or eliminating unsuccessful performers (even if some successful ones are also eliminated in this process). Statistical tables have been worked out that permit a selector to determine from his validity, selection ratio, and base rate how much improvement he can expect from the use of his test. These data tell him whether or not to use the test and what cut-off scores to set for acceptance or rejection of a candidate.[1]

Let us now look at two examples where a scientifically designed testing program and selection procedure has significantly improved the efficiency of the selection process. During World War II, the Air Force faced the problem of selecting from many candidates those who would most likely pass flight training and thus become successful pilots. Because it was expensive to bring a candidate into training who might "wash out" after some months, it was desirable to minimize wash-out rates. Psychologists designed a series of tests and developed a procedure for combining the scores into a single aptitude index which came to be known as the "pilot stanine" (stanines range from

[1] L.E. Albright, J.R. Glennon, and W.J. Smith give an excellent summary of this field in *The use of psychological tests in industry.* Cleveland: Howard Allen, 1963. See also Leona Tyler. *Tests and measurements.* Englewood Cliffs, N.J.: Prentice-Hall, 1963.

1 to 9; each unit is one-ninth of the total distribution). By successive refinement of this index (going repeatedly through the above steps), a useful predictor was eventually worked out.

The success of this predictor index can be judged from the results. Of all pilot trainees with a score of 1, 75 per cent were washed out of flight training; of all those with a score of 9, only 5 per cent were washed out. For scores in between, the wash-out rates were steadily higher as the stanine score became lower. It was clear that selection could be improved markedly by using the stanine measure in addition to or instead of whatever other procedures were currently in use.

A similar example can be cited from efforts to select life insurance salesmen by an aptitude index, again based on a whole range of tests. Of those men who scored very high on the index, 52 per cent survived with the company after one year and 30 per cent were considered successful in terms of sales; of those who scored low on the index, only 29 per cent remained with the company and only 11 per cent were considered successful.

Attempts have been made to predict performance in all kinds of industrial jobs, in schools and colleges, in the military services, and even in private mental clinics where admission may be based on predictors of the patient's "likelihood of responding to treatment." In most instances, some success has been achieved, but the practical problems of developing scientifically sound selection procedures sometimes outweigh the ultimate gains achieved. And, as we will see below, the whole procedure of selection based on testing may have organizational consequences not desired by the organization.

Variables may be observed in the context of an *interview* or a *standardized test situation,* may be elicited in response to questions on an *application blank,* or may be observed in a *job sample* where the applicant is actually asked to perform the work for a limited time. Which procedure is used in the total selection process depends upon a number of considerations. The reliability of the observations is crucial. One of the major reasons why tests are an important part of the selection procedure is that they can produce more standardized and hence more reliable responses than, for example, an interview. But answers elicited on an application blank or in an interview are in principle just as valuable as test scores, provided they can meet the criteria of reliability and precision. The kinds of variables which can be observed and measured in the effort to improve selection can range from obviously relevant ones (for example, the flight trainee's vision) to ones that may seem irrelevant but prove empirically to correlate with the criterion (for instance, the flight trainee's home town). The kinds of variables which can be observed fall into the following general classes. The methods which have proven to be helpful in assessing the variable are indicated in parentheses.

A. Biographical information and work-history (application blank, interview)

B. Intellectual level and aptitude (tests, job samples)

C. Specific areas of knowledge or specific skills (tests, job samples)

D. Attitudes and interests (tests, application blank, interview)

E. Motivation, personality, temperament (tests, interview)

In general, tests have proven to be most valuable in those situations in which the job to be performed can be clearly described and in which a clear-cut criterion of successful job performance exists. Thus, clerks, machine operators, and pilots have been generally easier to select by means of tests than teachers, managers, or salesmen.

The use of tests has not been limited to selection. There are organizational situations where a given group of employees must be assigned to a given group of jobs and the problem is to get the best fit between the people and the jobs. In this case, differential predictions must be made among the candidates rather than individual predictions for each one. Tests have also been used to assess the general potential for advancement of present employees. And tests have aided counseling psychologists in locating possible sources of tension or maladjustment. For example, tests may reveal that a given worker has been asked to do a job which is beyond or too far beneath his intellectual level.

Problems of Selection and Testing

The successful development of a useful test-and-selection procedure depends on a number of circumstances which are in practice difficult to deal with. Since jobs have become more complex and interdependent, particularly with the advent of automation, it is increasingly difficult to develop adequate job descriptions and adequate criteria of performance. Yet without a knowledge of what he is trying to predict, a psychologist cannot even begin to develop an effective predictor; without clear criteria of who did how well as a function of test scores, the tester cannot determine whether his test, no matter how valid it *seems* to be, is in fact an improvement over previously used selection procedures.

A second, related problem is that the ratio of management personnel to hourly paid workers has been steadily rising. This change has made it increasingly important to improve selection devices for managers, yet it is the managerial job which is most difficult to describe and analyze clearly. Many companies are investing great time and effort in developing tests to hire managers at various levels but with relatively little success. Many other companies use complex assessment programs run either by their own staffs or by consulting firms that specialize in such activities, but few data are available on the success of these programs.

A third force which undermines the effectiveness of job description and criterion development is the fluidity of jobs themselves in our rapidly changing technology and society. What may serve as a good description today, enabling the tester to select people validly, may in fact be irrelevant tomorrow. For many years, organizations were finding it useful to hire engineers and managers on the basis of *specific* technical courses which they had had in college. Today the rate at which engineers become "obsolete" is so great that companies are beginning to favor college students who have had more *general* educations, who have a solid background in pure mathematics, and who are generally better prepared to cope with a *changing* environment.

Fourth, the kinds of criteria which are applied to job performance tend to be short-run rather than long-run because the tester cannot wait forever before he checks the validity of the test. To the extent that short-run performance is itself highly correlated with long-run performance, this procedure is perfectly acceptable. But on many kinds of jobs and for most kinds of people, the *correlation between short-run and long-run performance tends to be low*: The person who is a good apprentice machinist may not do well when he is in charge of the machine; the good worker may not make a good group member when the job later requires teamwork; the good subordinate may not be effective as a supervisor, and so on.

The reasons for this low correlation are several: (1) A person often redefines a job in subtle ways that make a later measure meaningless because the performance criteria are no longer comparable from one person to the next. For example, two managers with identical formal responsibilities may develop quite different strategies of doing their job, one working on a refinement of task procedures while the other establishes good working relations with people. Performance measures of these people should take into account the strategies each has adopted if good predictions of future performance are to be made, even if the actual output of the departments is identical. (2) The person starts in one kind of job but later moves to another in which his task is different from what it was in the first job. (3) The longer the person remains in the organization, the more diverse his value is likely to become—he may be a terrible machine operator (for which the test may have been designed) but prove to be an excellent leader and organizer; if the test had eliminated him from one area, the organization might have lost a valuable resource in another area. (4) The person is more likely to be highly motivated to prove himself in the short run thus giving a biased picture of his long-run motivation. If the development of the test is a long-run proposition because the nature of the work is likely to remain static for some period of time, these difficulties can be overcome. They are acute, however, in a rapidly changing technology.

Specialists in personnel selection have attempted to overcome these various problems by developing more sophisticated and refined techniques of establishing criteria, by using multiple criteria in which different factors are given appropriate weights, by taking into account broad measures of performance which include loyalty to company and low absenteeism, by using more refined statistical procedures such as multi-variate analysis and multiple correlation, and so on. But the ultimate problem of finding predictors which will correlate with criteria remains the same.

Another problem with the traditional approach to selection is the questionable assumption that an applicant can be placed into a standard kind of test situation. People are dynamic creatures in constant interaction with their environment. In practice, therefore, standardized performance is difficult to obtain. First, a person may simply refuse the test. Second, he may, for any of a number of reasons, attempt to fake the test. He may fail in presenting an inflated picture of himself, but he may well succeed in rendering the test useless as a measure of his actual potential. Third, the person may resent the whole testing procedure. A classic example occurred some years ago when a well-meaning tester developed a "stress interview" designed to determine how the candidate would handle emotionally difficult situations. The real test consisted of the candidates being told, after many hours of paper-and-pencil tests, that he had failed them all. The purpose was to determine how the candidate would react to failure. The candidate who was most promising handled the failure experience adequately, whereupon he was congratulated and told that he had passed all of the selection criteria. He thanked the tester very much, told him that he was taking a job with another company which did not feel it necessary to put its employees through demeaning and traumatic application procedures, and walked out!

Perhaps the most serious problem with the selection-through-testing approach is that the individual tends to be viewed as a static entity to be measured, classified, and fitted into an organizational slot. Lip service is paid to his needs and motives, but the emphasis first and foremost is on the fulfillment of the organization's needs. As the field of selection has developed and become refined, these assumptions have remained essentially unchanged. Several consequences follow from them. First, an organization builds up an image of itself through the manner in which it recruits and selects its members. An applicant may well come to view himself as part of a mechanical, impersonal system which cares little for his needs and dignity. If he develops such an image of the organization, it may well undermine his long-run contribution in creativity and work effectiveness. Instead, he may become the good but apathetic worker, carefully keeping his real self-involvement out of the picture.

Second, through its selection policies the organization may reinforce what is already a powerful stereotype among the public at large that it is all-powerful, impersonal, and callous. For example, in a recent rebuttal of an attack by psychologists that personnel men continue to rely too much on the interview even though it has little validity for selection, a member of a personnel department in a large company defended the continued use of it on the grounds that it was *good public relations*. In a way, he was saying that the selection process should use methods which make the applicant feel worthwhile, even if the method is not valid, thus highlighting the company's need to present itself as human.

Finally, some people have even posed the ethical question of whether it is legitimate to use tests which probe the personal life of the applicant, sometimes without his knowledge, since good tests often disguise their purpose. This objection raises the whole issue of the ethical limitations of the psychological contract between employee and organization. Does the organization have the right to probe for personal facts in making its decisions about selection? If so, since the organization has available to it certain private facts about him, what implications does this have for an employee's later career development? Some psychologists have argued that the only person who should see the test data is the person himself. He should then be encouraged to share the data with the company, but at his initiative and under his control. This logic would apply especially to the personality assessments which are made of higher-level managers. The argument does not apply, however, to initial selection of employees.

None of these points argues that selection and testing should be stopped. However, it is important to recognize the consequences of using this approach because of both the assumptions to which it commits the organization and the image of the organization which it creates. These assumptions and images may well make it impossible for the organization at a later time to demand of its employees behavior based on other assumptions. Or, worse, the organization may bring into itself exact replicas of what it already has, losing the potential innovators and rebels who may become more important to organizational survival in a changing environment.

I will elaborate on these points at the end of this chapter after we have discussed both the human-engineering approach and training. For the present, I would simply like to stress that it is important to recognize the consequences for the total organizational system of the manner in which people are first brought into it.

JOB DESIGN AND HUMAN ENGINEERING

Another approach to solving the problem of recruitment and allocation is to design the job to fit the man. Where the selection approach is ultimately based on finding the right man for a given job, the job-design or human-engineering approach is ultimately based on the assumption that work should, from the outset, be explicitly set up to take into account the potentialities and limitations of the worker. And if the job is not suited for human performance in the first place or if a machine can do the job better, in the interests of over-all organizational effectiveness, a person should not be expected or allowed to do it. Adherents of both the human-engineering approach and the selection approach are committed to the ultimate assumption that the first requirement to be met is effective task performance. They disagree only on how one best accomplishes this end. (Employee needs are taken into account in the sense that a person placed into a job which he is unsuited for will be unhappy. But the organization and the selection specialist clearly retain control over the decision of who will be happy in which job. In this sense, task performance and meeting *organizational* needs remain the ultimate considerations.)

Historically, the job-design approach has been embodied in the work of industrial engineers or psychologists doing time-and-motion studies of workers. Time-and-motion studies involve the careful observation of a good or "standard" worker, recording the various moves he makes in performing his job, clocking the amount of time taken by each movement, and constructing a logical analysis of the job. This was done for one or more of the following purposes: (1) redesigning the job in order to make the movements simpler and quicker to do; (2) developing more efficient patterns of movement to be taught to workers so that they can do the job faster and with less fatigue; (3) setting standards for given jobs to be used as a basis for determining pay scales and criteria for the evaluation of any given worker; and (4) developing a complete job description to aid in the process of recruiting and selecting new workers, orienting them to their duties, and training them.

Thus, the industrial engineer contributed greatly to the whole "rationalization" of work upon which much modern industry depends. Important inventions like the assembly line, the setting of wage scales for jobs based on a rational assessment of the skills and training involved, and the development of machines and work layout which the average person could use efficiently grew partly out of this approach. To a large extent, it helped to replace the potentially biased and fallible judgment of the owner-manager with objective

Recruitment,
Selection,
Training,
and Allocation

standard procedures in job design, wage administration, and employee evaluation.[2]

At the same time, the classical industrial-engineering model has proven to have serious limitations and has created some unanticipated consequences for the effective utilization of workers. These problems stem from still another assumption traditionally made in both the selection and industrial-engineering approach. This assumption is that *the relevant unit of analysis is the individual worker.* What both approaches have failed to recognize is that formal organizations tend to breed informal organizations within them, and that *in the informal organization, workers and managers are likely to establish relationships with each other which will influence the manner in which they carry out their jobs or fulfill their roles.*

To elucidate this point, we must examine an important piece of history in the field of organizational psychology—the classic studies carried out by Mayo, Roethlisberger, and Dickson in the Hawthorne plant of the Western Electric Company in Chicago, Illinois.

The Hawthorne Studies [3]

In the late 1920's a group of girls who assembled telephone equipment were the subjects of a series of studies undertaken to determine the effect on their output of working conditions, length of the working day, number and length of rest pauses, and other factors relating to the "nonhuman" environment. The girls, especially chosen for the study, were placed in a special room under one supervisor and were carefully observed.

As the experimenters began to vary the conditions of work, they found that with each major change, there was a substantial increase in production. Being good experimenters, they decided, when all the conditions to be varied had been tested, to return the girls to their original poorly lighted work benches for a long working day without rest pauses and other amenities. To the astonishment of the researchers, *output rose again, to a level higher than it had been even under the best of the experimental conditions.*

At this point, the researchers were forced to look for factors other than those which had been deliberately manipulated in the experiment. For one thing, it was quite evident that the girls developed very high morale during the experiment and became extremely motivated to work hard and well. The reasons for this high morale were found to be several: (1) The girls felt special because they had been singled out for a research role; this selection showed that management thought them to be important.[4] (2) The girls

---

[2] I have not presented a detailed review of how job analysis, job evaluation, and job design are carried out because the technical complexity of these specialties lies beyond the scope of this book. For good accounts, you should consult R.M. Barnes. *Motion and time study.* New York: Wiley, 1958.

[3] The original description of these researches was published in F.J. Roethlisberger, and W.J. Dickson. *Management and the worker.* Cambridge, Mass.: Harvard Univ. Press, 1939. For a good analysis of the results in terms of a theory of group functioning, consult G.C. Homans. *The human group.* New York: Harcourt, Brace & World, 1950, Chapters 3 to 6.

[4] Working extra hard because of the feeling of participating in something new and special has come to be known as the "Hawthorne effect."

developed good relationships with one another and with their supervisor because they had considerable freedom to develop their own pace of work and to divide the work among themselves in a manner most comfortable for them. (3) The social contact and easy relations among the girls made the work generally more pleasant.

A new kind of hypothesis was formulated out of this preliminary research. The hypothesis was that motivation to work, productivity, and quality of work all are related to the nature of the *social* relations among the workers and between the workers and their boss. In order to investigate this more systematically, a new group was selected. This group consisted of 14 men: Some wired banks of equipment which others then soldered and which two inspectors examined before labeling it "finished." The men were put into a special room where they could be observed around the clock by a trained observer who sat in the corner of the room. At first the men were suspicious of the outsider, but as time wore on and nothing special happened as a result of his presence, they relaxed and fell into their "normal" working routines. The observer discovered a number of very interesting things about the work group in the bank-wiring room.

Result 1.   Though the group keenly felt its own identity as a total group, there were nevertheless two cliques within it roughly corresponding to those in the front of the room and those at the back. The men in front felt themselves to be of higher status and they thought that the equipment they were wiring was more difficult than that of the back group. Each clique included most of the wiremen, soldermen, and inspectors in that part of the room, but there were some persons who did not belong to either clique. The two cliques each had its own special games and habits, and there was a good deal of competition and mutual ribbing between them.

Result 2.   The group as a whole had some "norms," certain ideas of what was a proper and fair way for things to be. Several of these norms concerned the production rate of the group and could best be described by the concept of "a fair day's work for a fair day's pay." In other words, the group had established a norm of how much production was "fair," namely 6000 units, a figure which satisfied management but was well below what the men could have produced had fatigue been the only limiting factor. Related to this basic norm were two others: "one must not be a rate-buster," which meant that no member should produce at a rate too high relative to that of the others in the group, and "one must not be a chiseler," which meant that one must not produce too little relative to the others. Being a deviant in either direction elicited kidding rebukes, social pressure to get back into line, and social ostracism if the person did not respond to the pressure. In that the men were colluding to produce at a level below their capacity, these norms taken together amounted to what has come to be called "restriction of output."

The other key norm which affected working relationships concerned the inspectors and the supervisor of the group. In effect, the norm stated that "those in authority must not act officious or take advantage of their authority position." The men attempted to uphold the assumption that inspectors were no better than anybody else and that, if they attempted to take advantage of their role or if they acted officious, they were violating group norms. One inspector did feel superior and showed it. The men were able to play tricks on him with the equipment, to ostracize him, and to put social pressure of such an extent on him that he asked to be transferred to another group. The other inspector and the group supervisor were "part of the gang" and were accepted for this reason.

Result 3.   The observer discovered that the group did not follow company policy on a number of key issues. For example, it was forbidden to trade jobs because each job had been rated carefully to require a certain skill level. Nevertheless, the wiremen often asked soldermen to take over wiring while they soldered. In this way, they relieved monotony and kept up social contacts with others in the room. At the end of each day, each man was required to report the amount of work he had done. Actually the supervisor was supposed to report for all the men, but he had learned that the men wished to do their own reporting and decided to let them do it. What the men actually reported was a relatively standard figure for each day, in spite of large variations in actual output. This practice produced a "straight line output," a standard figure for each day. Actually, however, the output within the group varied greatly as a function of how tired the men were, their morale on any particular day, and many other circumstances. The men did not cheat in the sense of reporting more than they had done. Rather, they would underreport some days, thus saving up extra units to list on another day when they had actually underproduced.

Result 4.   The men varied markedly in their individual production rates. An attempt was made to account for these differences by means of dexterity tests given to the men. Dexterity test results did not correlate with output, however. An intelligence measure was then tried with similar lack of success. What finally turned out to be the key to output rates was *the social membership in the cliques*. The members of the high-status clique were uniformly higher producers than the members of the low-status clique. But the very highest and very lowest producers were the social isolates, who did not belong to either group. Evidently the individual output was most closely related to the social membership of the workers, not to their innate ability.

The output rates actually were one of the major bones of contention between the two cliques because of the pay system: Each man got a base rate plus a percentage of the group bonus based on the total production. The high-status clique felt that the low-status one was chiseling and nagged them about it. The low-status group felt insulted to be looked down upon and realized that the best way to get back at the others was through low production. Thus, the two groups were caught in a self-defeating cycle which further depressed the production rate for the group as a whole.

Conclusion.   What this study brought home to the industrial psychologist was the importance of the *social* factor—the degree to which work performance depended not on the individual alone, but on the network of social relationships within which he operated. As more studies of organizations were carried out, it became highly evident that informal associations and groups are to be found in almost any organizational circumstances and that these profoundly affect the motivation to work, the level of output, and quality of the work done. The Hawthorne studies were one of the major forces leading to a redefinition of industrial psychology as industrial *social* psychology. Although the Hawthorne studies showed clearly the existence of an informal social organization and its effects on work performance, it was not clear from these studies whether such an informal organization served any important functions for the workers. Might it not have been possible for management simply to tighten up on the men, enforce the rules, and shift them around or isolate them? Attempts to change the informal organization were not systematically made in the Western Electric Company, but cases from other organizations showed what some of the effects were if such changes were attempted. One of the best examples of these was provided by the Tavistock Institute studies of the effects of a technological change in the coal-mining industry in Great Britain.

The Tavistock Institute Coal-Mining Studies [5]

Eric Trist and his associates did extensive studies of the effects on coal miners of a technological change involving the installation of mechanical coal-cutting equipment and conveyors. The old system involved small groups ranging in size from two to eight men who worked as a highly interdependent team, usually in isolation from other similar teams. The team generally consisted of one skilled worker, his mate, and several laborers who removed the coal in "tubs." Each team had a small section of the coal-face and was responsible for the cutting, loading, and removal of the coal from its section (shortwall method). Teams were highly autonomous; members were picked by the team leader on the basis of mutual compatibility, and long-term relationships were established among members, relationships which included taking care of a team member's family if he was hurt or killed. Because of the anxieties aroused by working underground and in the dark, and because of the actual dangers involved in mining, strong emotional bonds formed among team members.

Conflict and competition between teams were common and various sorts of bribery and graft were involved in getting good sections of the coal-face to work and in acquiring enough "tubs" to be able to take out more coal than other teams. Although fights both underground and in the community were common, they apparently served as a useful outlet for the aggressions which resulted from the highly frustrating aspects of the work itself. The competition was accepted as part of life and did not disturb the basic social system of the community and the mine.

Because of the variable thickness of the coal seams in the British mines, it became desirable from an engineering point of view to install mechanical equipment for cutting and removing coal (longwall method). The kind of worker group needed for this type of operation differed sharply from what was needed for the shortwall method. The organization had to shift from

[5] These studies are reported in E.L. Trist and K.W. Bamforth. Some social and psychological consequences of the longwall method of coal-getting. *Human relations,* 1951, 4, 1–38. Also E.L. Trist *et al. Organizational choice.* London: Tavistock Publications, 1963.

Recruitment,
Selection,
Training,
and Allocation

small teams to large groups resembling small factory departments. These new groups consisted of 40 to 50 men under a single supervisor. Where previously the traditional groupings had been small teams and a total community, now an intermediate-size social system had to fulfill the various needs of the workers.

This intermediate-size system created great social difficulties because the men were generally spread out as wide as 200 yards, in a tunnel two yards wide and one yard high, and they were divided into three shifts. The task required such a high degree of coordination among the shifts and among the men within a shift, that an inefficiently done job anywhere along the line reduced the output of the entire group sharply. Particularly sensitive was the relationship between those men who had to prepare the face by drilling and blasting the coal loose and those men who then removed it on to the mechanical conveyor. The new small groups which emerged around common tasks were differentiated in terms of the kind of work and the kind of prestige they enjoyed in the total community. Thus, not only were communications between shifts undermined by the new method, but the new small-group organization was also similarly undermined by the differential prestige associated with the different work.

Besides the emotional strains which resulted from the disruption of group relationships with the advent of highly differentiated, rigidly sequenced, mechanical mass production methods came other problems having to do with the amount and quality of the work itself. Because the workers were so spread out, no effective supervision was possible. Because of the inherent dangers in the work situation and the inherent difficulties of the work itself (without opportunities to release tension in close emotional relationships), the productivity of the men tended to suffer. A norm of low productivity tended to arise as the only way to cope with the various difficulties encountered. Psychologically, the consequences were a loss of "meaning," an increasing sense of "anomie" (of being unrelated to others and to society), and a sense of passivity and indifference.

The important lesson in this example is that a technological change dictated by rational engineering considerations disrupted the social organization of the workers to such an extent that the new mechanical system could not work efficiently. The new formal organization was physically arranged in such a way that it was impossible for the men to form a meaningful informal organization which could meet their emotional needs. Only as the coal-mining industry, with the help of social scientists, began to redesign the formal organization as well as the organization of work, was it possible to begin to overcome some of the difficulties created.

The results I have cited in these two examples are typical of what has been found in company after company when jobs have been redesigned without explicit consideration of the consequences of the redesign for the social relationships among the workers. It has been learned over and over again that the informal organization does play a key role in meeting important emotional needs of the organization member and therefore cannot be ignored or "forbidden."

As research results have accumulated, a gradual change has taken place in the traditional concept of job design and industrial engineering. The original assumption that the layout of the work was to be dictated largely in terms of engineering principles has gradually been replaced by a more refined concept of human engineering which takes the *interaction* and *mutual influence* of the man and the machine or the man and the job as its basic point of departure. The recognition that workers bring to the job social needs which become expressed in informal social groupings has led to more careful strategies of job design and greater care in introducing changes which disrupt existing relationships. The degree to which social relationships were found to influence productivity and the way in which work was actually carried out has led to a greater concern with human relations.[6]

For example, in a recent experiment, a small electronics firm called Non-Linear Systems, Inc. attempted to allow the work to be organized primarily in terms of the skills and social needs of the workers.[7] Instead of imposing a rational division of labor on the workers, management invited them to work out with their supervisors an arrangement which would best meet their own emotional and social needs as well as be efficient. The system they devised takes advantage of the particular talents of the workers but is flexible enough so that job trading and other forms of work exchange make the whole work pattern more meaningful to them. Each member of the team develops identification with the whole product. This identification has led to much-higher-quality standards than those previously attained with a system of outside inspectors, partly because the product is now seen by each member as "his own baby."

The type of reorganization exemplified in Non-Linear Systems has often been labeled as *job enlargement* in contrast to *job simplification*. Instead of attempting to locate the minimum specialized unit of work and assigning it to one expert to do over and over again, the procedure is to ask how much of the total job any particular individual can really become involved with. Enlarging the scope of the job increases motivation, sense of meaning and identification with the work, and sense of autonomy. To the extent that the typical worker has needs for meaning and autonomy, job enlargement and similar concepts would appear to come closer to creating what industrial psychologists were after in the first place—work conditions which lead to effective job performance. Whereas they started to look for those conditions in the physical environment, they found them in the social environment and in the relationship of workers to their jobs.

A *Final Issue*

In describing problems with the selection-and-testing approach, I pointed out that one of the consequences is that the organization creates a certain image of itself in the mind of a new employee. The assumptions underlying the traditional industrial-engineering approach led to practices which would build a similar image. Specifically, the employee may well feel himself to be part of a big machine into which he is fitted or which is impersonally fitted to some of his skills and

[6] How this concern expressed itself in management philosophy will be explored in the next chapter. Our focus here remains on job design and human engineering.

[7] A. Kuriloff. An experiment in management—putting Theory Y to the test. *Personnel,* 1963, Nov.–Dec., 8–17.

limitations. There is an implication of almost a complete denial that he may have needs other than that of performing the organizational role exactly as specified. At best, the organization presents itself as being indifferent to such needs.

A potential problem both for the organization and the employee lies in the fact that the employee comes to accept this image as the reality and learns to behave accordingly. As Chris Argyris and Douglas McGregor have argued, the employee learns to do exactly what the organization expects and nothing more.[8] In fact, for a variety of emotional reasons, he will tend to find the lowest limit of performance that the organization will tolerate and will exercise his creativity and expend the major portions of his energy either outside the organization or in attempts to defeat the organization. Thus, in the bank-wiring-room, great effort went into working out systems by which variable production could be presented to management as straight-line production, and great creativity was exercised in learning how to meet production standards with a minimum of effort.

If workers adapt to organizations in this manner—and there is evidence that they do—a serious problem arises for the organization if, at any point, it becomes more dependent on the worker for greater productivity, loyalty, or creativity. If the company's competitive situation worsens or technological changes require new products and new processes, the organization may need the help of its own employees. Unfortunately, if it has trained them to be indifferent and apathetic, it is unlikely to be able to elicit their cooperation. Even if the employees have information that would be of value to management, they would be unlikely to share it because of their image of the organization as basically exploitative and indifferent to human needs. Even if they could work harder, it is not likely that management could invent any incentive to get them to do so. Only by proving to employees that the organization does indeed care for their social and emotional needs could such commitment be elicited. Unfortunately, there are many cases where an organization not only is unaware of the kind of image its practices are creating in the minds of its members, but is also unprepared to accept the consequences of such images as determiners of how individual employees will relate themselves to the organization.

In summary, I have argued that the selection and engineering approach rest on certain assumptions about people which are communicated to new employees of organizations through the practices of recruitment, selection, and job placement. Some of these assumptions deny certain emotional and social needs which an employee brings with him, leaving him in the situation of having to find satisfactions either in informal organizations or, if this is impossible, outside the organization; the consequence is that he becomes either alienated from the organization or passively resistant to it. This is not to say that selection methods and industrial engineering should therefore be abolished and replaced by other methods which may be less efficient. I am saying, though, that organizations should recognize the consequences of their own approaches and practices, and decide whether to use them partly

[8] C. Argyris. *Personality and organization.* New York: Harper, 1957. D.M. McGregor. *The human side of enterprise.* New York: McGraw-Hill, 1960.

on the basis of their willingness to accept these consequences. I am arguing for developing a greater awareness of the complex interrelationships between organizational practices and members' attitudes.

Let us look next at the third of the traditional methods of bringing people into organizational roles—training.

TRAINING

Once you have rationally defined the organizational mission, have designed the jobs which must be fulfilled to achieve it, and have recruited and selected the appropriate people to do the jobs, there still remains the problem of properly training these people. Training has become all the more important as jobs have become technically more complex and specialized and as organizations have become more highly differentiated. Thus, to become an effective member of an organization requires not only the learning of job skills but also an understanding of the organizational mission, its ways of doing things, its climate or culture, and the various career paths available within it. Training broadly conceived can thus aid in (1) orienting and indoctrinating a new employee; (2) teaching him the specific knowledge, skills, and attitudes he will need to perform the job; and (3) providing opportunities for education and self-development which will make it possible for the employee to rise successfully within the organization.

The basic logic of training can be described in terms of the following steps:

1. Identify the training needs or goals. This step assumes that a clear concept exists of the knowledge, skills, or attitudes which the trainee is supposed to acquire during the training period, and that these fit somehow with the demands of the particular job or the needs of the organization in general.

2. Select the appropriate target group for training.

3. Design the training experiences in terms of the appropriate learning theory, taking into account the nature of what is to be learned and who the learners are. A program of changing attitudes of managers does not necessarily operate according to the same learning theory as a program of teaching unskilled workers how to run a lathe.

4. Evaluate the outcomes of training with a scientifically designed evaluation scheme. For example, the evaluation design should involve observation of the trainees back on the job at some period of time after training and should, if possible, involve a control group to determine whether changes observed are, in fact, attributable to the training effort.

The kinds of learning principles which should be taken into account in designing a training program have been derived from many decades of research on human and animal learning. A sample of such principles is presented below.

Learning will be facilitated to the extent that:

1. The learner is motivated to learn.

2. The responses to be learned are meaningfully related to each other and to the motives which the learner brings with him.

3. The new responses to be learned do not conflict with old responses or attitudes; if they do, learning will be facilitated to the extent that the training provides an opportunity for the old responses to be unlearned before the new responses are learned.

4. The new responses can be successfully generalized from the learning situation to other situations and can be appropriately used.

5. The new responses are "reinforced" in the sense of being followed by some reward or information that the response has been made correctly.

6. The learner is an active participant in the learning process, trying out new responses, rather than a passive listener only.

7. The learning situation provides opportunities to practice the new responses and allows for "plateaus," periods of little improvement which often precede marked improvement.

8. The new responses to be learned are broken up into learnable units, and presented in an appropriately paced sequence.

9. Coaching or guidance is available to help the learner develop new responses.

10. The learning situation allows for individual differences in the speed of learning, the depth of learning or amount learned, and the sequence in which responses are learned.

The translation of principles such as these into concrete training programs for particular purposes has required great skill and ingenuity on the part of training designers. In particular, it has not been easy to do so for the more complex kinds of educational or self-development activities which have come to be labeled management development; in these, the *relearning* of *attitudes* and *motives* is more important than the learning of knowledge and skills.

Training programs for new members of organizations are the rule rather than the exception. Whether the problem is to teach a new nurse the particular workings of the hospital she has joined, a recruit how to be an effective combat soldier, a worker how to run a machine, a teacher how to use a particular method in vogue in a school system, or a management trainee how to supervise more effectively, some form of training activity is likely to be used. Most organizations have departments which are responsible for training new members and providing continuing training or educational opportunities for regular members.

Because our society is changing so rapidly, there is a constant problem of obsolescence. The knowledge and skills which are valuable today may not be valuable in five years. Rather than firing people who are obsolete, more and more organizations are attempting to retrain them to provide the new skills necessary to keep up with new technology and new organizational demands. Successful training programs exist for almost any kind of concrete skill needed, from driving a truck and running a machine to selling and the general skills of how to handle people, whether they be customers, fellow workers, or subordinates.

Problems of Training

Training programs are effective to the extent that the logical steps cited above can be carried out in practice, particularly that the principles of the learning theory can be met. In general, the more specific and concrete the training goals are, the more successful the training is likely to be. Thus, teaching a new employee how to run a particular piece of machinery, or how to fill out forms in his department, or how to repair equipment, is likely to be more successful than teaching him the company philosophy (which many orientation programs attempt to do), how to develop new attitudes toward people (which may be necessary in order to take on supervisory responsibility), or how to sell a complex product.

Training efforts are vulnerable to some of the reactions which may be aroused by selection and job placement procedures. Here again, I am trying to illustrate how the subsystems of an organization interact. For example, if the testing and hiring procedure convinces new employees that the organization is impersonal and callous, they may well approach orientation training with a defensive or apathetic attitude, thus violating one of the key learning principles, namely that the learner be motivated to learn. Or, if the recruitment procedure promises that the new employee will be given a challenging and meaningful job, yet he finds himself in a training situation which may last anywhere from two weeks to one year, he may become disaffected and mistrustful of the organization as a whole and therefore resist the training.

The problem just described is particularly common in the early job experiences of college graduates. Follow-up research of persons with B.A.'s and M.A.'s and of graduates of business schools indicate that their important motives are to test themselves in a working situation and to discover for themselves what their worth is in the "world of work." [9] Recruitment practices promise the graduate jobs with great responsibility and challenge attached to them. These jobs sound as if they would provide the kind of test the graduate is seeking. Then if the organization puts the individual in a training program in which (1) he does not have any real responsibility, (2) he is put back into a situation which resembles the school atmosphere from which he has sought relief, and (3) he is prevented from testing and validating himself, he may well become disaffected and leave the organization.

The high turnover in the first few years among college graduates entering industry is largely attributable to just such psychological forces. The important point is that there may be nothing wrong with the training program as conceived. The problem lies rather in the failure to see the interaction between the training program, the needs of the people, and the recruitment and selection practices. The interaction between training and other organizational forces is particularly clear where new attitudes and perceptions are involved. In the next section dealing with supervisory training, I will elaborate upon this point.

[9] E.H. Schein. How to break in the college graduate. *Harvard Business Review*, Nov.–Dec., 1964, 68–76.

The more psychologists
and sociologists actually studied the behavior of people in organizations, the
clearer it became that their performance was critically related to the quality
of their interpersonal relationships. In particular, their relationship with
their supervisors came to be seen as central. As the Hawthorne studies had
foreshadowed, if workers feel that their boss does not act too officious, does
not interfere too much with social relationships built up on the job, and does
not demand production in an impersonal and callous way, they will not only
feel better but will *work more effectively*. From these early findings there derived many hundreds of studies which attempted to locate the specific traits of
the good supervisor. As such characteristics were identified, efforts were made to
train existing supervisors to exhibit them to a greater degree.

For example, in study after study, it became clear that if a supervisor
showed some concern or consideration for his employees as human beings,
if he was to some degree "employee-centered," his subordinates were more
productive than average. We will examine findings such as these in greater
detail in the following chapter. For our purposes here, the important point
is that as such a trait was identified, it seemed perfectly logical to set up a
training program to teach supervisors to develop that trait.

The same logic, when applied to managers in general, led to a conception
of *management* training. A present or future manager could, it was assumed,
learn the various responses and characteristics desirable in a manager. Thus,
he could learn to understand the different functions of a business such as
finance, production, marketing, and accounting; he could learn how to get
along well with superiors, peers, and subordinates; he could learn how to
make decisions quickly and effectively without having full information on
which to base these decisions; he could learn how to get others to carry
out decisions, how to delegate work to them, how to motivate and stimulate
others to maximum performance, and how to see each job through to com-
pletion.

The kind of training needed to teach these different abilities must, of
course, be varied, but the assumption that they all can be taught was
generally not questioned seriously. Even though many of the things to be
taught involved new attitudes, new perceptions, and possibly even new
motives, psychologists set about to train managers in these skills with the
same enthusiasm they used when teaching motor skills or specific areas of
information. With the beginning of research on training, however, some of
the difficulties with the original assumptions were revealed.

To illustrate the kinds of problems which supervisory training ran into,
we need to look at two studies.

The International Harvester Supervisory Training Program.[10]   The International Harvester Company decided to train foremen in leadership principles and techniques in a two-week course run at their central training

[10] E.A. Fleishman. Leadership climate, human relations training, and supervisory behavior. *Personnel Psychol.*, 1953, 6, 205–222.

facility. Edwin Fleishman, a psychologist, developed several tests to determine what kinds of effects the training program had on the attitudes and behavior of the participating foremen. These tests were given to the foremen immediately before and after training as well as at intervals ranging from two to 39 months later. In addition, the tests were given to the superiors of the trainees as well as to samples of their subordinates.

The tests were scored on two qualities which were shown statistically to represent most of the kinds of leadership behavior exhibited and which were independent of each other: *consideration*—the degree to which the foreman was sensitive to and considerate of the feelings of the men under him; and *initiating structure*—the degree to which the foreman was concerned about task performance by planning, organizing work, setting schedules, initiating ideas, and so on.

The first important finding of the study, reminiscent of the Hawthorne study results, was that the foremen's scores on these dimensions did not correlate with age, background, or other personal factors. They did correlate, however, with the kind of behavior exhibited by their own bosses. Those men who worked under considerate bosses were reported to be more considerate by their own subordinates than those men who worked under less considerate bosses. The same chain reaction was found for their initiating-structure quality.

The second finding concerns the immediate effects of training. Following the course, the foremen rated significantly higher in consideration and significantly lower in initiating structure than before, a result generally in line with the training course objectives. However, the purpose of any training program is not merely to produce temporary effects. Fleishman studied various groups of foremen at various times following the training and compared them with a control group which had received no training.

The findings of this part of the research were dramatic and unexpected. Not only did the trained foremen revert to their original behavior and attitudes, but on consideration, they ended up showing *less* consideration than the control group, and on structuring, they ended up showing *more* structuring than the control group.

To discover what might have caused this boomerang effect, Fleishman studied the behavior and attitudes of the bosses of the trainees and found that they tended on the average to be higher in structure than the foreman group and that there was a distinct relationship between the attitudes of the boss and those of the trained foremen, even after training. The only foremen who were more considerate following the training period were those who worked under bosses who were themselves highly considerate. In other words, *the effects of training were intimately related to the culture, or climate, of the departments from which the men came.* These climates had as much of an effect on the trainee as did the training. Consequently, the training was effective, in terms of its own goals, only in those departments in which the climate from the outset supported the training goals.

A Case of Conflict Resulting from Supervisory Training.   An even more dramatic example of the relationship between training and other organizational variables was recently reported by Sykes.[11] A medium-sized contracting firm called in management consultants to increase the general efficiency of the company. The consultants recommended that training be instituted for all supervisors and that a similar course be given to management. The consultant was called in to run the training program, which emphasized lectures on good business practices and sound human relations combined with group-participation discussions and training in becoming more effective in groups. This format stimulated frank exchanges of opinions and feelings, and more active participation by the trainees.

The sessions were at first formal but soon loosened up and provided an opportunity for the supervisors to express certain grievances about the company which they had until then only discussed with close friends or held back altogether. Company practices were unfavorably compared with ideal ones as outlined in the lectures. Most of the grievances concerned the behavior of senior management. Almost all the groups who went through the training unanimously decided that senior management should make certain fundamental changes in their attitudes and behavior, and that if they did not do so then, with the impetus of an outside consultant, they would never change.

The various grievances were compiled into a report which the consultant submitted to the managing director. It was then decided that the same course should now be run for higher levels of management and that the grievance report should be used as material in the course. It developed in the discussions that senior and junior management both felt that neither the consultant nor the supervisors really understood the practical difficulties they encountered in management. Many of the grievances leveled at them were accepted by senior management but felt to be the fault of junior management. Junior managment agreed with the grievances, accepted some blame themselves, but laid most of it on senior management. They frequently attacked senior management for having had bad relations with staff men in the past.

The managing director was left with the conclusion that no blame attached to himself. Following the rather unsuccessful management course, he announced a number of decisions which had been based on recommendations made by the consultant in line with foremen grievances. These involved adjustments of pay, institution of a better system of communications with supervisors, a shorter work week, greater opportunities for promotion from within the company by advertising the jobs internally, and so on. The reaction of the supervisors was, "We'll wait and see." Shortly after this, the consultant terminated his relationship with the company, having completed his job.

Supervisors suspected that senior management had not really changed their attitudes and this suspicion was borne out by the slowness with which the decided-upon changes were instituted. Only after a period of months were some of the changes made and some of these were made grudgingly.

About one or two months after the training course, foremen started to leave the company. During the year after the course, 20 per cent of the 97

---

[11] A.J.M. Sykes. The effect of a supervisory training course in changing supervisors' perceptions and expectations of the role of management. *Human Relations,* 1962, 15, 227–43.

supervisors left and another 25 per cent began to look for jobs elsewhere. In previous years, no more than one or two men had left per year.

An investigation of who left and why revealed three factors. Among the foremen who left there was (1) a high proportion of intelligent men; (2) a high proportion of men with relatively few years of service, although even among men with over 10 years of service, 39 per cent were dissatisfied (left or tried to leave); and (3) a very high percentage of men who had regular contact with senior management. Apparently this last factor was most important, in that it revealed directly to the foremen how little attitude change had actually occurred among senior management.

In summary, what started out to be a management-improvement effort led in the course of one year to a severe conflict between first-line supervisors and senior management, resulted in no change in management attitudes, but produced a high rate of turnover among some of the very men whom the company needed to keep. What the organization and the consultant had failed to foresee was the complex relationships among the several subsystems of the organization—the foreman group, junior management, senior management, and the managing director. Had the training course been adequately thought out in terms of its potential effects on these various subsystems, the disastrous effects might have been avoided.

Summary and Conclusions

I have tried to bring out in the above examples that the initial logic of training has in it some pitfalls, just as the initial logic of selection and of job design has in it some pitfalls. In the case of training, three major problems can be identified: (1) The outcome is often not clearly specifiable, not because of insufficient study of the job for which a person is to be trained, but because the trainee sometimes is expected to grow and develop in terms of his general attitudes, his basic capacities, and general knowledge *in order to prepare him for an uncertain future.* (2) The training itself unleashes some forces within the organization which produce pressures toward change in other parts of the organization, changes which those parts may not be prepared to cope with. (3) The training effort interacts with recruitment, selection, and job design, as previously noted.

In reference to the first point, it is increasingly clear that because of rapid technological change jobs and roles in organizations are becoming, on the one hand, more complex and, on the other hand, more diffuse and uncertain. The typical training effort therefore faces the problem not only of how to teach a new employee the specifics of a complex job for today, but also how to create a learning situation in which that employee can develop his other capacities by way of preparing for an uncertain future. In management training, the latter factor is paramount. While it may be possible to specify what a machine operator needs to learn and to mold trainees to this image, it is becoming increasingly difficult to specify what a manager should learn and increasingly questionable whether a manager can be molded or trained. Instead, there is an increasing tendency to view the problem as one of providing opportunities for *self*-development, determining what sorts of human potential emerges, and then allocating people in terms of their potentials. This concept is obviously very different from that of specifying jobs and molding people to them.

The second problem mentioned above, that of generating unforeseen consequences, was well illustrated by Sykes in his study of a particular supervisory program. The dilemma which this example poses can be described as follows. It has been found that for human relations training to be effective in changing trainee attitudes, skills, and overt behavior, it is necessary to use *participative* techniques. The trainee must get involved, must expose some of his present attitudes and behavior, must get reactions to these, and must practice alternate attitudes and behaviors before any real change in him occurs. It has also been found that such training occurs best in group settings in which a number of trainees work together on their common human relations problems. The setting must be one in which support is given even when group members expose some of their weaknesses and problems. Such a climate in turn stimulates a more open, frank expression of feelings. In expressing their feelings, the trainees will inevitably share their views of the organization, their own bosses, and their feelings of satisfaction and dissatisfaction. As these feelings are shared, they take on increasing potency by virtue of being shared. The isolated gripe may have been suppressed because the person felt himself to be alone; but once the gripe is exposed he may discover that others feel like him which may lead to demands for something to be done about it.

Even the *possibility* of sharing can become a force influencing other parts of the system. A researcher goes into an organization to determine feelings about something or somebody. Nobody knows exactly what he found out, but everybody knows that at least in his report or in his mind there is a pooling of information which previously had been privately held. That it is pooled somewhere arouses the possibility of action being taken based on it and plants the idea that action is possible where it may never have been previously considered. Thus, the other horn of the dilemma is that the very climate which makes good training possible also brings with it forces toward change which the system must then cope with. *Good management training may, in other words, be inseparable from broader programs of organizational change and improvement.*

The points which I previously made about the dependence of the organization on its employees in a rapidly changing environment has obvious consequences for the training effort. Just as it is possible through selection and job design to create an image of a static organization into which people have to be "engineered," so it is possible through systematic indoctrination and training to finish the job of molding them to the organization. Traditional organization theory requires just such a sequence. Clearly define the job, select your employees in terms of the relevant capacities for the job, and train them to perform the job according to specifications. Following the training, employees are ready for assignment to fulfill their organization duties.

The assumptions underlying this approach are quite sound for many organizations and many types of jobs. They break down for more complex jobs and for managerial functions; they are inappropriate for organizations which find themselves in a rapidly changing environment, and they create a certain image of the organization which may have other human consequences not foreseen by the organization and not desired. In particular, they may make employees passive, indifferent, and uncommitted to organizational goals.

If full recognition is given to the interdependency between different parts of an organizational system, it must be in turn recognized that how the employee is trained and the assumptions underlying training will markedly affect his image of the organization and will directly affect other parts of the organizational system. The conclusion which follows is that the induction and utilization of people in organizations cannot be viewed in terms of the separate personnel functions traditionally defined. It makes no sense from this point of view to have highly specialized selection procedures, highly specialized job-design procedures, and highly specialized training procedures. It is far more important to see the interdependence of these functions and to plan in terms of an integrated conception of the organization and its mission. This will, in the long run, require systems-level theories which can predict some of the interrelationships between these functions which we traditionally tend to separate.

Organizational Man and the Process of Management

In order for an organization to fulfill its mission, the people who make it up must coordinate their efforts to make possible an outcome which the isolated individual would be unable to achieve alone. Thus, organizations are characterized by a *division of labor* and by some kind of *hierarchy*. Coordination through the decisions made by some members of the organization can be defined as the process of management. Those who have the power to make the decisions are called the managers. The others are usually called the "lower members" of the organization, the workers or subordinates. How an organization defines who shall manage

43

and who shall be managed, and by what system of authority is highly variable. Historically, we have seen autocratic organizations in which pure coercive power determined who controlled the behavior of others; we have also seen benevolent autocracies, paternalistic organizations, and egalitarian ones which deliberately distributed power widely among the members and used a rational-legal basis for authority. There is no one right way for organizations to be managed. Rather, it depends on historical circumstances, the actual mission of the organization, and, most importantly, the fit between management's assumptions about people and the actual characteristics of the organization members. Whether we are consciously aware of them or not, we all make assumptions about what people are like, what motivates them, and how therefore to deal with them. The manager's assumptions will not only determine to some degree the form of organization to be utilized in fulfilling a task, but will also determine his management strategy. The kinds of expectations he has about people, which make up his side of the psychological contract, will be primarily an expression of his assumptions about them.

But employees have expectations also. They make assumptions about the nature of organizations and expect organizations to behave in certain ways toward them. Therefore, the actual interaction between the employee and the organization can best be thought of as the working out of a *psychological contract* through what H. Levinson has called the process of *reciprocation*.[1] The organization does certain things to and for the employee and refrains from doing other things. It pays him, gives him status and job security, and does not ask him to do things too far removed from his job description. In exchange, the employee reciprocates by working hard, doing a good job, and refraining from criticizing the company in public or otherwise hurting its image. The organization expects the employee to obey its authority; the employee expects the organization to be fair and just in dealing with him. The organization enforces its expectation through the use of whatever power and authority it has. The employee enforces his expectations through attempts to influence the organization or by withholding his participation and involvement, as when he goes on strike or becomes alienated and apathetic. Both parties to the contract are guided by assumptions concerning what is fair and equitable.[2]

Historically, the nature of the psychological contract between organizations and their members has undergone a number of changes. These changes can best be understood in terms of a typology of organizations proposed by Amitai Etzioni.[3]

[1] H. Levinson. *Reciprocation: the relationship between man and organization.* Invited address, Division of Industrial and Business Psychology, Amer. Psychol. Assoc., Sept. 3, 1963. Sociologists speak of a "norm of reciprocity" (A.W. Gouldner. The norm of reciprocity. *Amer. Sociol. Rev.,* 1960, 25, 161–78) or principles of "distributive justice" in social relationships (G.W. Homans. *Social behavior: its elementary forms.* New York: Harcourt, Brace & World, 1961).

[2] E. Jaques. *Equitable payment.* New York: Wiley, 1961.

[3] A. Etzioni. *A comparative analysis of complex organizations.* Glencoe, Ill.: The Free Press, 1961.

Etzioni's typology is an attempt to provide a basis for classifying all kinds of organizations which exist within society. His basic variables are the type of power or authority which the organization uses and the type of involvement which the organizational member has with the organization. He distinguishes three types of organizations on the basis of (1) whether they exert *pure coercive* power, (2) whether they attempt to elicit involvement through the exchange of economic rewards for membership and performance based on *rational-legal authority,* or (3) whether they attempt to elicit involvement primarily on the basis of *normative rewards,* where membership or the opportunity to perform a function is intrinsically valued. Table 1 provides examples of the types of organizations which may be classed under each heading, as well as some mixed types.

TABLE 1

Classification of Organizations
Based on Type of Power or Authority Used

A. Predominantly *coercive* authority

    Concentration camps
    Prisons and correctional institutions
    Prisoner-of-war camps
    Custodial mental hospitals
    Coercive unions

B. Predominantly *utilitarian,* rational-legal authority, use of economic rewards

    Business and industry (with a few exceptions)
    Business unions
    Farmers' organizations
    Peacetime military organizations

C. Predominantly *normative* authority, use of membership, status, intrinsic value rewards

    Religious organizations (churches, convents, etc.)
    Ideologically based political organizations or parties
    Hospitals
    Colleges and universities
    Social unions
    Voluntary associations and mutual benefit associations
    Professional associations

D. *Mixed* structures

    Normative-coercive: combat units
    Utilitarian-normative: most labor unions
    Utilitarian-coercive: some early industries, some farms, company towns, ships

Based on A. Etzioni. *Op. cit.*

Etzioni distinguishes three types of involvement of organization members, as follows: (1) *alienative,* which means that the person is not psychologi-

Organizational Man and the Process of Management

cally involved but is coerced to remain as a member; (2) *calculative,* which means that the person is involved to the extent of doing a "fair day's work for a fair day's pay"; and (3) *moral,* which means that the person intrinsically values the mission of the organization and his job within it, and performs it primarily because he values it.

Table 2 shows the nine logical types of organizational relationships which could result from this typology. Etzioni points out, however, that the type of personal involvement possible depends to a large extent on the kind of power or authority used by the organization. Hence there is a tendency for organizations to cluster in certain cells of the table, primarily along the diagonal from upper left to lower right. Thus, if we look back at the examples in Table 1, we see that the kinds of organizations listed under coercive power tend primarily to have alienated members who would rather not belong but are coerced to remain; the kinds of organizations listed under utilitarian tend to have calculative members who expect primarily economic rewards for their performance but who do not feel they have to like their jobs or their employer; the kinds of organizations listed under normative tend to have members who belong because they value the goals of the organization and like to fulfill their organizational roles, that is, they consider it morally right to belong.

TABLE 2

Types of Power-Authority versus Types of Involvement

	Coercive	Utilitarian	Normative
Alienative	*		
Calculative		*	
Moral			*

Based on A. Etzioni. *Op. cit.*
* Represents the predominant types.

We can restate this point in our terms by saying that the organizational types which fall along this diagonal have workable and "just" psychological contracts with their members. What they get in the way of involvement is in line with what they give in the way of rewards and the kind of authority they use. If a utilitarian organization like a manufacturing concern expects its employees to like their work, to be morally involved, it may be expecting workers to give more than it gives them. Or if a normative organization like a university wishes to maintain the moral involvement of its faculty, it must use a reward-and-authority system in line with such involvement. If a university, for example, withholds status or privileges such as academic freedom and expects its faculty to obey arbitrary authority, it will be violating its psychological contract, resulting either in a redefinition of the contract (the faculty may redefine its role and change the nature of its involvement from moral to calculative, which would mean putting in minimum class and office hours based on the amount of pay received) or an alienation of the faculty (they may do the required amount of teaching and research, but without concern for quality and without enthusiasm).

The above typology represents "pure" types of organizations which seldom actually exist. Most organizations are a complex mixture of the types. Nevertheless, it is useful to describe the pure types and to consider the basic dimensions of type of authority-power and type of psychological involvement. It is useful, first of all, in giving us perspective. Historically, there has been a shift away from pure coercive and normative types of organization toward various combinations of utilitarian with either normative or coercive. Particularly in the development of business and industry, we have witnessed the movement from coercive companies, which could force labor to do what they wanted because of the scarcity of jobs and low standard of living in society, to companies that are concerned about providing adequate economic rewards, job security, and many other kinds of benefits to their employees. The growth of unions and collective bargaining has promoted the utilitarian, rational-legal type of contractual relationship between management and labor.

As business and industry have become more complex and more dependent on high-quality performance from both managers and workers, a trend has begun toward making the psychological contract more utilitarian-normative. By this I mean that companies are seeking to establish new kinds of relationships with their members. These new relationships to some degree abandon utilitarian conceptions in favor of normative ones. Members are increasingly expected to like their work, to become personally committed to organizational goals, and to become creative in the service of these goals; in exchange, they are given more influence in decision-making, thus reducing the authority of management.

The redefinition of the basic contract between man and organization reflects, at a psychological level, a change in the assumptions which have been made about the fundamental nature of man himself. In order to understand this trend, therefore, we must examine in greater detail the kinds of assumptions which managers and organization planners have made about man. The ultimate issue for the organizational psychologist is the degree of fit between such assumptions and what the research evidence has shown about the nature of man.

MANAGEMENT'S ASSUMPTIONS ABOUT PEOPLE

Every manager makes assumptions about people. Whether he is aware of these assumptions or not, they operate as a theory in terms of which he decides how to deal with his superiors, peers, and subordinates. His effectiveness as a manager will depend on the degree to which his assumptions fit empirical reality. Historically, the assumptions about people in organizations have largely reflected philosophical positions on the nature of man and have served as the justification for the particular organizational and political system of the time. The four sets of assumptions I will discuss are presented roughly in the order of their historical appearance: (1) rational-economic man; (2) social man; (3) self-actualizing man; (4) complex man.

Rational-Economic Man

The assumptions which underlie the doctrine of rational-economic man derived originally from the philosophy of hedonism, which argued that man calculates the actions that will maximize his self-interest and behaves accordingly. The economic doctrines of Adam Smith, which were built on this assumption, led to the theory that relationships in the market place between organizations and between customers and buyers should be left alone because the separate pursuits of self-interest would regulate market relationships adequately.

What this general line of thought led to in reference to employees can be described as follows:

a. Man is primarily motivated by economic incentives and will do that which gets him the greatest economic gain.

b. Since economic *incentives* are under the control of the organization, man is essentially a passive agent to be manipulated, motivated, and controlled by the organization.

c. Man's feelings are essentially irrational and must be prevented from interfering with his rational calculation of self-interest.

d. Organizations can and must be designed in such a way as to neutralize and control man's feelings and therefore his unpredictable traits.

Implied in these assumptions are some additional ones which have been made explicit by Douglas McGregor in his analysis of organizational approaches toward people.[4] He labels these additional assumptions as Theory X, in contrast to Theory Y which will be discussed later:

e. Man is inherently lazy and must therefore be motivated by outside incentives.

f. Man's natural goals run counter to those of the organization, hence man must be controlled by external forces to insure his working toward organizational goals.

g. Because of his irrational feelings, man is basically incapable of self-discipline and self-control.

h. *But,* all men are divided roughly into two groups—those who fit the assumptions outlined above and those who are self-motivated, self-controlled, and less dominated by their feelings. This latter group must assume the management responsibilities for all the others.

Ultimately, then, the doctrine of rational-economic man classified human beings into two groups—the untrustworthy, money-motivated, calculative mass, and the trustworthy, more broadly motivated, moral elite who must organize and manage the mass. As we will see, the main problem with this

[4] D.M. McGregor. *The human side of enterprise.* New York: McGraw-Hill, 1960.

theory is not that it fits no one, but rather than it overgeneralizes grossly and oversimplifies in painting man as either black or white.

Implied Managerial Strategy.   The kinds of assumptions a manager makes about the nature of people will determine his managerial strategy and his concept of the psychological contract between the organization and the employee. The above assumptions, for example, imply essentially a *calculative* involvement, in Etzioni's terms. The organization is buying the services and obedience of the employee for economic rewards, and the organization assumes the obligation of protecting itself *and the employee* from the irrational side of his nature by a system of authority and controls. Authority rests essentially in designated offices or positions and the employee is expected to obey whoever occupies a position of authority regardless of his expertise or personality.

Primary emphasis is on efficient task performance. Management's responsibility for the feelings and morale of people is secondary. The managerial strategy which emerges is well summarized by Koontz and O'Donnell in their four principal functions which the manager must perform—(1) plan; (2) organize; (3) motivate; and (4) control.[5]

If people are not producing or morale is low, the solution is to be sought either in the redesign of jobs and organizational relationships, or in changing the incentive and control system to insure adequate motivation and production levels. Thus, an industrial organization operating by these principles will seek to improve its over-all effectiveness by worrying first about the organization itself—who reports to whom, who does what job, are the jobs designed properly in terms of efficiency and economy, and so on? Secondly, it will re-examine its incentive plans, the system by which it tries to motivate and reward performance. If productivity is low, the company may well try an individual bonus scheme which rewards the high producer, or it may stimulate competition among workers and give special rewards to the winners. Thirdly, it will re-examine its control structure. Are supervisors putting enough pressure on the men to produce? Does the system adequately identify and punish the man who fails to produce, who shirks on the job? Are there adequate information-gathering mechanisms to enable management to identify which part of the organization is failing to carry its proper share of the load?

The burden for organizational performance falls entirely on management. Employees are expected to do no more than the incentive and control systems encourage and allow; hence, even if an employee did not fit the assumptions made about him, it is unlikely that he could express alternative behavior. Consequently, the greatest danger for an organization operating by these assumptions is that they tend to be self-fulfilling. If employees are expected to be indifferent, hostile, motivated only by economic incentives, and the like, the managerial strategies used to deal with them are very likely to train them to behave in precisely this fashion.

Evidence for Rational-Economic Man.   The best evidence for this image of man comes from our own day-to-day experience and most of the history of industry. The assumptions about man and the management principles which

[5] H. Koontz and C. O'Donnell. *Principles of management.* 3rd ed. New York: McGraw-Hill, 1964.

follow from them *work* in many different kinds of situations. For example, the concept of the assembly line as an efficient way to produce has proven itself over and over again. Money and individual incentives have proven to be successful motivators of human effort in many kinds of organizations. The fact that the employee's emotional needs were not fulfilled on the job was of little consequence because he often did not expect them to be fulfilled. He had learned from his parents what life in organizations was like and behaved accordingly.

Yet, in spite of the dramatic success of management strategies based on the rational-economic image of man, there were problems and instances of failure. If pay was the only thing workers could expect from the organization, then they wanted more of it. As the standard of living in industrial society rose, employees changed their expectations of what should be provided in the way of pay and privileges. Large industrial organizations initially found it easy to exploit workers; the exploitation led ultimately to the development of unions, however, which gave workers a more powerful tool for influencing management if their expectations were not met.

Jobs became more complex, and competition among organizations became more severe, which meant that management had to depend increasingly on the judgment, creative capacity, and loyalty of the worker. As organizations came to expect more of employees, they also had to re-examine their assumptions about them. And as organizations came to expect more, employees came to expect more as well. Thus, the nature of the psychological contract has tended to shift as organizations have become more complex and more dependent on their human resources.

At the same time, industrial psychologists and industrial sociologists began to study more carefully what the motivations and behavior patterns of organizational members actually were. As studies such as the Hawthorne series were conducted, it became clear that workers brought with them many motives, needs, and expectations which did not fit the rational-economic-man assumptions, yet which influenced the quality and quantity of their work and their relationship to the organization. These studies led to another set of assumptions which characterized what we may call the *social* man.

Social Man

In the previous chapter, we cited two studies which showed the importance of social motives in organizational life. The Hawthorne studies dramatically drew attention to the fact that in determining work patterns the need to be accepted and liked by one's fellow workers is as important as, or more important than, the economic incentives offered by management. They further showed that a man will resist being put into a competitive position with other men. He may well handle the threat which competition implies to the losers by banding together with others to resist the threat. Something akin to this happened among the coal miners studied by Trist.

For Elton Mayo, the evidence of the Hawthorne studies and the subsequent data obtained in interviews with workers were convincing proof that industrial life had taken the meaning out of work and had frustrated man's basic social needs.[6] In interviews, so many workers complained of a feeling of alienation and a loss of a sense of identity, that Mayo developed a set of assumptions about the nature of man which are quite different from those concerning rational-economic man:

a. Man is basically motivated by social needs and obtains his basic sense of identity through relationships with others.

b. As a result of the industrial revolution and the rationalization of work, meaning has gone out of work itself and must therefore be sought in the social relationships on the job.

c. Man is more responsive to the social forces of the peer group than to the incentives and controls of management.

d. Man is responsive to management to the extent that a supervisor can meet a subordinate's social needs and needs for acceptance.

Implied Managerial Strategy.   These assumptions have drastically different implications for management strategy from those involving rational-economic man. First, they dictate that a manager should not limit his attention to the task to be performed, but should give more attention to the needs of the people who are working for him. Second, instead of being concerned with motivating and controlling subordinates, the manager should be concerned with their feelings, particularly their feelings in regard to acceptance and sense of belonging and identity. Third, the manager should accept work groups as a reality and think about *group* incentives rather than individual incentives. Fourth, and most important, the manager's role shifts from planning, organizing, motivating, and controlling to acting as an intermediary between the men and higher management, listening and attempting to understand the needs and feelings of his subordinates, and showing consideration and sympathy for their needs and feelings. In terms of these assumptions, the initiative for work (the source of motivation) shifts from management to the worker. The manager instead of being the creator of work, the motivator, and the controller, becomes the facilitator and sympathetic supporter.

The kind of authority and the kind of psychological contract which these assumptions and managerial strategies imply are quite different from those which follow from traditional organizational assumptions. Perhaps most important is that the manager acknowledges the existence of needs other than purely economic ones. His authority is still based largely on his occupying an office or a position, but he does not exercise it simply on a man-to-man basis. Rather, he uses his authority to specify for the group what the goals should be, but then leaves the group some leeway about how best to accomplish the goals. His acknowledgement of social needs on the job opens the door to a psychological contract between the man and the organization in which each can expect much more of the other. If the employee can expect gratification of some of his important emotional needs through participation in the organization, he can to a degree become morally involved in the organiza-

---

[6] E. Mayo, *The social problems of an industrial civilization.* Boston: Harvard Univ. Grad. School of Business, 1945.

tion; for its part, the organization can then expect a greater degree of loyalty, commitment, and identification with organizational goals.

As Mayo and others after him have found, if management creates a situation for workers in which they feel frustrated, threatened, and alienated, they form into groups *whose norms run counter to the goals of management*. The men successfully meet their social needs but at the expense of management. If management can harness the group forces and get group norms working in the direction of organizational goals, a tremendous reservoir of energy and motivation becomes available. In terms of our typology, unless management can meet the social needs of workers, they will become alienated from the formal organization, but *morally* involved with the informal organization. On the other hand, according to these assumptions, if management can meet social needs, it can get workers morally involved with the formal organization and its goals.

Evidence for Social Man.   Beyond the classic studies of Mayo, Roethlisberger, and Trist, there are several strands of research evidence which are consistent with the assumptions outlined above.

One line of evidence comes from observational studies of different kinds of work groups in different organizational settings. For example, Zalesnik and his co-workers found the following results in a department of some 50 workers in a medium-sized manufacturing concern: (1) both productivity and satisfaction of the workers were unrelated to the pay and job status which the individual received, but were related to group membership; (2) regular group members tended to be satisfied and to conform to the group norms of productivity as well as to management's expectation; (3) deviants and isolates tended to be less satisfied and to violate group norms; (4) deviants and isolates who aspired to group membership and identified with the group tended to produce below the group's norms; (5) deviants and isolates who did not aspire to group membership tended to produce above the group's norms.[7]

In a study of human relations in restaurants, Whyte found that social and group factors related significantly to absenteeism, quitting work, and the quality of customer service.[8] If the group was well knit and integrated and if the supervisor permitted such group formation to occur, relations within the group and the quality of work were good. If the requirements of work upset group relations, however, a variety of troubles arose. For example, if low-status workers like waitresses were put into the position of initiating the actions of higher-status workers like cooks (by shouting orders to them, for example), conflict, resistance, and poor service resulted. When a system of writing out orders and simply depositing them within reach of the cook was instituted, service improved because cooks could now accept orders at their own pace and on their own initiative.

Seashore studied the relationship between group cohesiveness, as measured by responses to a questionnaire, and a variety of other factors in a heavy

[7] A. Zalesnik, C.R. Christensen, and F.J. Roethlisberger. *The motivation, productivity, and satisfaction of workers: a prediction study.* Boston: Div. of Research, Harvard Business School, 1958.

[8] W.F. Whyte. *Human relations in the restaurant industry.* New York: McGraw-Hill, 1948.

machinery company.[9] He found that high group cohesiveness was associated with high productivity if the group members had high confidence in management and with low productivity if the group members had low confidence in management. Also, persons in high-cohesiveness groups were less likely than those in low-cohesiveness groups to feel "jumpy," or "nervous," or under pressure.

Studies of assembly lines and mass production have consistently shown that the major source of worker dissatisfaction is the disruption of social relations, the inability to talk comfortably and at his own initiative with his neighbor, and the inability to pace social contacts in terms of his own needs.[10] On the other hand, where work has been redesigned in such a way as to facilitate teamwork and social interaction, it has proven to increase both productivity and morale.[11]

Studies of combat in World War II and in the Korean conflict further underlined the importance of social relations. Not only was it found that the major source of motivation to fight was a soldier's sense of commitment to his fellow soldiers, particularly those with whom informal relationships had arisen, but emotional breakdown in combat also proved to result from feelings of having let down a fellow soldier. Rehabilitation of men with such emotional problems could be facilitated at the front lines by talking out the problems in the small group which had shared the stresses with the emotionally disturbed person. Evacuating him tended to increase emotional difficulties by heightening the soldier's already great sense of guilt that he had "let his buddies down."

A very important series of studies by Whyte attempted to test the assumption that money is indeed a prime motivator of productivity in industrial settings.[12] Through observing work groups, interviewing productive and unproductive workers, and studying the backgrounds of high and low producers, he obtained the following results:

1. Among production workers, the proportion of men who are primarily motivated by money is very low; perhaps as few as 10 per cent of workers will respond to an individual incentive scheme and ignore group pressures to restrict output.

2. When an incentive scheme works, whether it is an individual or group incentive, it often works for reasons other than making more money. In fact, (a) workers may perceive the meeting of production goals to be a sort of game which one can win or lose; they work hard because the game is fun; (b) workers may work to meet higher quotas in order to maintain good relations with their supervisor or to minimize the pressure for production from him; and (c) working at a brisk pace is often less boring or fatiguing than

[9] S.F. Seashore. *Group cohesiveness in the industrial work group.* Ann Arbor: Survey Research Center, Univ. of Michigan, 1954.

[10] F.J. Jasinski. Technological delimitation of reciprocal relationships: a study of interaction patterns in industry. *Human Org.,* 1956, 15, No. 2. C.R. Walker and R.H. Guest. *The man on the assembly line.* Cambridge, Mass.: Harvard Univ. Press, 1952.

[11] A.K. Rice. *Productivity and social organization: the Ahmedabad Experiment.* London: Tavistock Publications, 1958. E. Trist *et al. Op. cit.*

[12] W.F. Whyte. *Money and motivation: an analysis of incentives in industry.* New York: Harper, 1955.

an erratic or slow pace. Not all of these factors argue for the social-man theory, but they clearly indicate the inadequacy of the rational-economic-man theory.

3. "Rate-busters" who produce above the group norms differ in their background and personality from "restricters" who work at the level of group norms. The rate-busters are most individualistic, come from homes in which economic individualism is highly prized (such as a farm family), and do not seem to have strong social needs; restricters come from urban working-class homes, value cooperation and getting along with others, and have stronger social needs as evidenced by a higher rate of joining outside social groups. From these studies, we have evidence that at least some workers fit the social-man assumptions but that perhaps here also, the problem is overgeneralization. Not all workers have the same social needs.

The gains to be achieved from group incentive plans which harness group forces toward organizational goals can be seen in some companies that have adopted the Scanlon Plan.[13] This plan was developed by Joseph Scanlon after many years of working in industry and observing the weaknesses of individual incentive schemes, of suggestion plans to get workers' ideas on improvement of production methods, of profit-sharing plans to give workers a sense of identity with their company, and so on. Scanlon was intuitively very sophisticated about learning theory and about the social needs of workers. To meet the social needs, he decided that suggestions for improvement of work procedures should be submitted to committees consisting of both management and workers, and that individual credit for the suggestion should be played down. If a suggestion was adopted, however, and actually reduced the costs of production, the savings should be returned to the workers as soon as possible, and as a percentage of their base pay rather than a flat bonus.

In terms of learning theory, workers could see, under the Scanlon Plan, an immediate connection between their own efforts and the economic rewards they obtained as a group. They obtained immediate knowledge of results. In the typical profit-sharing plan, the worker rarely sees how his bonus is related to his own efforts. In the typical suggestion plan, most individuals will not submit key suggestions because they do not wish to be singled out from their group and because they recognize that ideas are usually a joint product of the efforts of many. The Scanlon Plan overcame both of these difficulties by distributing savings to the group. The evaluation committees not only provided their members with immediate gratification of social needs but also led to improved communication between management and the workers and greater involvement of workers in organizational activities.[14]

A different line of evidence for the importance of social needs comes from studies of leader-follower relations or superior-subordinate relations. We have previously described Fleishman's study of supervisory behavior and his finding that the showing of consideration to subordinates was related to their

[13] F. Lesieur. *The Scanlon Plan.* New York: Wiley, 1958.

[14] The success of the Scanlon Plan in raising productivity and reducing costs has been very great in some organizations and very small in others. I do not mention it here as valid evidence for social-man theories, but as an ingenious application to management of these assumptions.

productivity and morale. Similar evidence comes from a whole series of studies carried on by the Institute of Social Research at the University of Michigan.[15] In studies of clerical workers, for example, it was found that departments with supervisors who were primarily *production-oriented* tended on the average to produce less than departments with supervisors who were *employee-centered*.

The major differences between the two types of supervisor were the following: Production-centered supervisors tended to be authoritarian, arbitrary, defensive, and resistant to influence; they gave detailed supervision on what to do and how to do it; if things were not being done right, they might step in and do it themselves. The employee-centered supervisors tended to be cooperative, democratic, amenable to influence, and more reasonable; they gave subordinates a general outline of what was to be done and how to do it without detailed instructions or detailed checking on how the work was going; they assumed that the workers were responsible, as indeed turned out to be the case. The production-centered supervisor ignored the social and personal needs of his employees while the employee-centered supervisor was sensitive to them and dealt with them rather than ruling them out of order. As was found in Fleishman's studies, there was considerable evidence that a supervisor's style and assumptions also reflected those of his own boss.

In another study, the leadership style was deliberately varied to determine the effects on productivity. This study showed that production-centered approaches could increase productivity as much as employee-centered approaches but only at the expense of the human organization. In other words, the production-centered groups achieved high short-run productivity but in the long run stimulated the formation of antimanagement groups of the sort we have previously discussed. The employee-centered groups harnessed the social motivation to organizational goals and could therefore count on a continued high rate of productivity.[16]

The Michigan studies also uncovered several other phenomena which complicate the picture. In a study of a large trucking company, Vroom and Mann found that the nature of the job being performed influenced the workers' preference for type of supervision.[17] Package handlers whose work was highly *interdependent* showed a preference for employee-centered supervision; truck drivers and dispatchers whose work was highly individual and *independent* preferred a more production-centered, authoritarian approach by dispatchers which maximized efficiency of communication. Vroom has also found that the individual worker's personality affects his preference for and response to the type of supervisor. Those men who were themselves dependent, authoritarian types preferred that sort of supervision and responded well to it; those men who were highly independent were more productive when they were allowed to participate in decisions by more employee-centered supervisors.[18]

---

[15] R. Likert. *New patterns of management.* New York: McGraw-Hill, 1961.

[16] Nancy Morse and E. Reimer. The experimental change of a major organizational variable. *J. abnorm. soc. Psychol.,* 1956, 52, 120–129.

[17] V.H. Vroom and F.C. Mann. Leader authoritarianism and employee attitudes. *Personnel Psychol.,* 1960, 13, 125–140.

[18] V.H. Vroom. *Some personality determinants of the effects of participation.* Englewood Cliffs, N.J.: Prentice-Hall, 1960.

Out of the Michigan studies has come a very important theoretical concept which reflects the social-man theory of people in organizations. The concept is that organizations are not sets of relationships among people, as depicted in the typical organization chart, but rather are relationships among sets of interlocking and interdependent groups. Thus, the president and his immediate subordinates make up the top group. The subordinates make up a peer group which overlaps the top-management group. Each vice-president is the top man of a group composed of himself and his immediate subordinates, who, in turn have their own peer groups. If one is to understand the motives of people in organizations, one must, according to this view, consider the various group memberships. Those people who belong to several groups—for instance, a vice-president who is part of top management but also the head of his own department—is called by Likert a *linking pin,* in that he joins the various groups together. It is the linking pins who occupy key roles in organizations in terms of serving as the channel of communication and influence from one group to another.

To summarize, many studies lend support to the assumptions that man is essentially socially motivated in his organizational life. To the extent that these assumptions are empirically valid, they imply that members not only can but do seek to be morally involved in the organizations to which they belong. If this proves to be generally true in many kinds of organizations, it undermines the very concept of the utilitarian organization which can establish a psychological contract based purely on economic rewards and rational bargaining. But the research findings caution us not to overgeneralize. Though the rational-economic model of man clearly is not very general, we cannot claim clear evidence for the universality of social man either.

Self-Actualizing Man

A number of psychologists studying human behavior in organizations have come to Mayo's conclusion that organizational life, particularly in industry, has removed meaning from work. This loss of meaning is not related so much to man's *social* needs, however, as to man's inherent need to use his capacities and skills in a mature and productive way. For Argyris, Maslow, McGregor, and others who tend toward this point of view, the problem is that most jobs in modern industry are so specialized or fragmented that they neither permit the worker to use his capacities nor enable him to see the relationship between what he is doing and the total organizational mission.[19] The kinds of assumptions which are implied about the nature of man can be stated as follows:

a. Man's motives fall into classes which are arranged in a hierarchy: (1) simple needs for survival, safety and security; (2) social and affiliative needs; (3) ego-satisfaction and self-esteem needs; (4) needs for autonomy and independence; and (5) self-actualization needs in the sense of maximum use of

[19] C. Argyris. *Integrating the individual and the organization.* New York: Wiley, 1964. A. Maslow. *Motivation and personality.* New York: Harper, 1964. D.M. McGregor. *Op. cit.* The assumptions described here are similar to what McGregor calls Theory Y, though actually Theory Y would be a blend of these assumptions and those taken up in the *next* section.

all his resources. As the lower-level needs are satisfied, they release some of the higher-level motives. Even the lowliest untalented man seeks self-actualization, a sense of meaning and accomplishment in his work, if his other needs are more or less fulfilled.

b. Man seeks to be mature on the job and is capable of being so. This means the exercise of a certain amount of autonomy and independence, the adoption of a long-range time perspective, the development of special capacities and skills, and greater flexibility in adapting to circumstances.

c. Man is primarily self-motivated and self-controlled; externally imposed incentives and controls are likely to threaten the person and reduce him to a less mature adjustment.

d. There is no inherent conflict between self-actualization and more effective organizational performance. If given a chance, man will voluntarily integrate his own goals with those of the organization.

Implied Managerial Strategy.   If a manager has assumptions such as these, he will use a strategy similar to that derived from the social-man theory but with additional features. For one thing, he will worry less about being considerate to employees and more about how to make their work intrinsically more challenging and meaningful. The issue is not whether the employee can fulfill his social needs; the issue is whether he can find in his work meaning which gives him a sense of pride and self-esteem.

The manager may find himself often in the role of interviewer, attempting to determine what will challenge a particular worker. He will be a catalyst and facilitator rather than a motivator and controller. Above all, he will be a delegator in the sense of giving his subordinates just as much responsibility as he feels they can handle.

The implications for authority and the psychological contract which derive from these assumptions are most important. First of all, authority shifts from being in the office or in the man to being basically in the task itself. The manager is the agent through whom task requirements are communicated, but if man responds to challenge, seeks autonomy, and is capable of disciplining himself, he himself (the subordinate) will see to it that the task is adequately performed. The whole basis of motivation shifts from being *extrinsic,* in that the organization does something to arouse motivation, to being *intrinsic,* in that the organization provides an opportunity for the employee's existing motivation to be harnessed to organizational goals.

In both classical and social-man theories, the psychological contract involves the exchange of extrinsic rewards (economic ones or social ones) for performance. In the self-actualizing-man theory, the contract involves the exchange of opportunities to obtain intrinsic rewards (satisfaction from accomplishment and the use of one's capacities) for high-quality performance and creativity. This, by definition, creates a moral rather than a calculative involvement, and thus releases a greater potential for commitment to organizational goals and creative effort in the pursuit of those goals. The employee has much greater influence if he is granted a certain amount of autonomy in doing his job, while the manager must give up certain of his traditional prerogatives, particularly in the area of control. Therefore, an organization which is operating according to these assumptions will have a much broader power distribution or will tend toward what Leavitt has called "power equalization." [20]

Evidence for Self-Actualizing Man.   Mayo's original interviews with employees of the Hawthorne plant and of other companies he studied were actually as much evidence for man's need to find challenge and meaning in his work as they were evidence for social needs. Argyris in is studies of various kinds of manufacturing organizations has found again and again that if the job itself thwarts an employee in being too limiting or meaningless, he will create meaning and challenge in outwitting management or in banding together with others in groups.[21] Fantastic creativity has been observed over and over again among production workers when they develop fancy rigs to make their work a little easier or develop complex schemes to enable them to avoid working. The interesting feature of these activities is that they often involve greater expenditure of energy than doing the job set by management would require. The willingness to expend energy to find something meaningful, even if it is only a poor joke on management, testifies to the strength of the need for meaning. Assembly lines and mass production systems destroy social relations, but even more importantly, they often take meaning and challenge out of work.

The evidence is not clear, though, about what meaning and challenge in his work the lower-level employee or the less-educated person in our society expects to find. It may be that for many members of organizations, it will be sufficient to establish an essentially calculative-utilitarian contract with the organization: "a fair day's work for a fair day's pay." In this instance, the worker is working to make enough money to find meaning and challenge *off* the job. If the organization can function effectively with this degree of involvement, there is no problem. However, a number of organization theorists, notably Argyris, have argued that this compromise is a waste of human resources and that if organizations could make work more meaningful, they could elicit greater involvement, and thereby greatly improve their over-all effectiveness.

The model of self-actualizing man becomes most relevant if one considers the motivation of managers, professional employees, and, generally, more highly educated groups in our society. For example, in a study of accountants and engineers, Herzberg and his associates found clear evidence for the importance of these factors.[22] They asked each of their respondents to describe what was going on when they were feeling both particularly good and particularly bad about their jobs. Then they coded the various responses and classified them into general categories such as factors relating to accomplishment, salary, security, and so on.

Herzberg and his colleagues found that what the men mentioned when they said they felt good about their jobs, factors which were genuine

[20] H.J. Leavitt (ed.). *The social science of organization: four perspectives.* Englewood Cliffs, N.J.: Prentice-Hall, 1963.

[21] C. Argyris. *Integrating the individual and the organization.* New York: Wiley, 1964.

[22] F. Herzberg, B. Mausner, and B. Snyderman. *The motivation to work.* New York: Wiley, 1959.

motivators, invariably had to do with accomplishments and the feeling of growth in job competence. What made these men feel good was clearly related to self-actualization. What made them feel bad about the jobs, on the other hand, were the background or surrounding factors such as inadequate salary, poor working conditions, insufficient job security, poor supervision, and so on. Herzberg called these *hygienic* factors. If they did not reach a certain minimum condition, a person would be unhappy. But they were not capable of eliciting positive motivation and a feeling of well-being. Such a feeling could come only with genuine accomplishment on a meaningful and challenging task.

As the number of well-educated and semi-professional employees in organizations has increased, the importance of true motivators has increased because of the high cost of having an upper-level employee be unproductive. Studies of scientists in research organizations have confirmed the findings that productivity and creativity are strongly related to challenge, job accomplishment, and autonomy.[23] Some degree of autonomy is probably crucial because it permits a person to set some of the dimensions of his task and thus to provide for himself an appropriate level of challenge.

Looking back at other findings from this perspective suggests the possibility that genuine motivators were not found in the early industrial studies because even the hygienic conditions were insufficient to permit genuine motivation. As long as workers felt threatened, insecure, underpaid, and poorly supervised, they had to cope with these factors. Perhaps only as such factors have reached minimum standards has it been possible to discover that the important motivators lie above and beyond job conditions—they concern the basic nature of the job itself. Even the Michigan studies of employee- versus production-centered supervision are perhaps more relevant to self-actualization than to social needs in that the employee-centered supervisor, by setting goals and then leaving subordinates alone, was providing greater challenge and autonomy to them.

Looking again at companies that have used the Scanlon Plan, it is clear that once employees do become committed to organizational goals, they are capable not only of much more production but also of innovations which reduce costs often beyond the best efforts of industrial engineers.

In summary, the assumptions underlying the concept of self-actualizing man place emphasis on higher-order needs for autonomy, challenge, and self-actualization, and imply that such needs exist in all men and become active as lower-order security and social needs come to be satisfied. There is clear evidence that such needs are important in the higher levels of organizational members like managers and professionals on the staff. It is not clear how characteristic these needs are of the lower-level employee, although many of the problems which were interpreted to be examples of thwarted social needs could as easily be reinterpreted to be instances of thwarted needs for challenge and meaning.

In the case of those workers who are *not* actively seeking challenge or self-actualization at the place of work, either this need is lacking or it is not given

[23] D. Pelz and F.M. Andrews. Organizational atmosphere, motivation, and research contribution. *Amer. Behav. Scientist,* 1962, 6, 43–47.

an opportunity to express itself. This last may occur because lower-order needs are not yet fulfilled or the organization has "trained" workers not to expect meaning in their work as part of the psychological contract.

Complex Man

Organization and management theory has tended toward simplified and generalized conceptions of man. Empirical research has consistently found some support for the simple generalized conception, but only some. Consequently, the major impact of many decades of research has been to vastly complicate our models of man, of organizations, and of management strategies. Man is a more complex individual than rational-economic, social, or self-actualizing man. Not only is he more complex within himself, being possessed of many needs and potentials, but he is also likely to differ from his neighbor in the patterns of his own complexity. It has always been difficult to generalize about man, and it is becoming more difficult as society and organizations within society are themselves becoming more complex and differentiated.

What assumptions can be stated which do justice to this complexity?

a. Man is not only complex, but also highly variable; he has many motives which are arranged in some sort of hierarchy of importance to him, but this hierarchy is subject to change from time to time and situation to situation; furthermore, motives interact and combine into complex motive patterns (for example, since money can facilitate self-actualization, for some people economic strivings are equivalent to self-actualization).

b. Man is capable of learning new motives through his organizational experiences, hence ultimately his pattern of motivation and the psychological contract which he establishes with the organization is the result of a complex interaction between initial needs and organizational experiences.

c. Man's motives in different organizations or different subparts of the same organization may be different; the person who is alienated in the formal organization may find fulfillment of his social and self-actualization needs in the union or in the informal organization; if the job itself is complex, such as that of a manager, some parts of the job may engage some motives while other parts engage other motives.

d. Man can become productively involved with organizations on the basis of many different kinds of motives; his ultimate satisfaction and the ultimate effectiveness of the organization depends only in part on the nature of his motivation. The nature of the task to be performed, the abilities and experience of the person on the job, and the nature of the other people in the organization all interact to produce a certain pattern of work and feelings. For example, a highly skilled but poorly motivated worker may be as effective *and satisfied* as a very unskilled but highly motivated worker.

e. Man can respond to many different kinds of managerial strategies, depending on his own motives and abilities and the nature of the task; in other words, there is no one correct managerial strategy that will work for all men at all times.

Implied Managerial Strategy. If assumptions such as the above come closer to the empirical reality, what implications do these have for managerial strategy? Perhaps the most important implication is that *the successful man-*

ager must be a good diagnostician and must value a spirit of inquiry. If the abilities and motives of the people under him are so variable, he must have the sensitivity and diagnostic ability to be able to sense and appreciate the differences. Second, rather than regard the existence of differences as a painful truth to be wished away, he must also learn to value difference and to value the diagnostic process which reveals differences. Finally, he must have the personal flexibility and the range of skills necessary to vary his own behavior. If the needs and motives of his subordinates are different, they must be treated differently.[24]

It is important to recognize that these points do not contradict any of the strategies previously cited. I am not saying that adhering to traditional principles of organization, or being employee-centered, or facilitating the work of subordinates is wrong. What I am saying is that any of these approaches may be wrong in some situations and with some people. Where we have erred is in oversimplifying and overgeneralizing. As empirical evidence mounts, it is becoming apparent that the frame of reference and value system which will help the manager most in utilizing people effectively is that of science and of systems theory. If the manager adopts these values toward man, he will test his assumptions and seek a better diagnosis, and if he does that he will act more appropriately to whatever the demands of the situation are. He may be highly directive at one time and with one employee but very nondirective at another time and with another employee. He may use pure engineering criteria in the design of some jobs, but let a worker group completely design another set of jobs. In other words, he will be flexible, and will be prepared to accept a variety of interpersonal relationships, patterns of authority, and psychological contracts.

Evidence for Complex Man. In a sense, all of the researches previously cited support the assumptions stated in this section, but it will be helpful to review and to cite some additional studies which highlight human complexity and human differences. For example, both Whyte and Zalesnik in the studies previously cited showed that the background and pattern of motivation of rate-busters differed from that of underproducers. Both types were group deviants, but the reasons why one group was indifferent to group sanctions while the other group aspired to membership and was rejected were found in their different personal and social backgrounds.

The study of Vroom and Mann which was cited on page 55 showed that workers with different personalities preferred different leadership styles in their bosses. A similar example drawn from another type of organization, namely the prison, comes from Grusky's study.[25] Because the prison is a coercive organization which forces its inmates to be totally dependent and submissive, it should create primarily alienative involvement. Grusky hypothesized and confirmed that those prisoners who had submissive and dependent kinds of personalities would be relatively less alienated, more cooperative, and

[24] Theorists like Argyris, Likert, and McGregor have argued for more diagnostic ability and skill-flexibility in managers. My argument here summarizes theirs and attempts to make it more explicit and general. A similar analysis and generalization has also been made by W.G. Bennis in Revisionist theory of leadership. *Harvard Business Review,* 1961, 39, 26 ff.

[25] O. Grusky. Authoritarianism and effective indoctrination: a case study. *Adm. Sci. Quart.,* 1962, 7, 79–95.

more positive about prison life. Both Pearlin [26] and Argyris [27] in studying the alienation of workers in typical industrial organizations found cases of workers who were not alienated because their personal needs and predispositions made them comfortable in a highly authoritarian situation which demanded little of them, either because they did not seek challenge and autonomy or because they genuinely respected authority and status.

In a recent study of four types of industrial workers, Robert Blauner [28] found evidence for very different patterns of alienation depending on the nature of the technology which was involved in the work. He defined alienation as being the resultant of four different psychological states which are in principle independent of each other: (1) sense of powerlessness or inability to influence the work situation; (2) loss of meaning in the work; (3) sense of social isolation, lack of feeling of belonging to an organization, work group, or occupational group; and (4) self-estrangement or sense that work is merely a means to an end, lack of any self-involvement with work.

Automobile workers on assembly lines were found to be alienated by all four criteria mentioned. At the other extreme, members of the printing trades felt a sense of influence, meaning, integration into the occupational group, and deep involvement in their work. Textile workers resembled automobile workers but were highly integrated into communities in which the traditional values taught them not to expect a sense of influence or meaning. These values in combination with paternalistic management practices made them feel reasonably content with their lot in spite of strong forces toward alienation. The fourth group, chemical workers, represented still another pattern. Because the continuous processes in chemical plants tend to be highly automated, the chemical worker has a great deal of responsibility for controlling the process, considerable autonomy and freedom, a close sense of integration with others on his shift and in the plant, and high involvement in the work because of the high responsibility. The variation in these four types of workers illustrates the danger of generalizing about alienation among factory workers, and the utility of more refined concepts of alienation and technology such as Blauner has developed.

Studies of the dominant motivational patterns which led men into management positions show similar variations. Although there is some agreement that managers, in comparison to other groups of similar socio-economic status or to other occupations, are more concerned with power, achievement, income, and advancement, the variability within each occupational group is more striking than the difference between occupational groups. For example, in reviewing the literature Vroom finds that sales and personnel managers are more likely to have strong social or affiliative needs, while production managers tend to have strong needs to work with mechanical things. Higher levels of management are more likely to be concerned with desires for personal growth and needs for self-actualization and autonomy than lower levels of management.[29]

[26] L.I. Pearlin. Alienation from work. *Amer. Sociol. Rev.*, 1962, 27, 314–326.
[27] C. Argyris. *Op. cit.*
[28] R. Blauner. *Alienation and freedom.* Chicago: Univ. of Chicago Press, 1964.
[29] V.H. Vroom. *Motivation in management.* New York: Amer. Foundation for Management Research, 1964.

Gellerman, in discussing varieties of motives such as the ones mentioned, has pointed out that even economic rewards can and do have vastly different meanings to different people.[30] For some people, money represents basic security and love; for others, it represents power; for still others, it is a measure of their achievement in society; and for still others, it represents merely the means to the end of comfortable and sumptuous living. Thus it is difficult to judge, even in the case of a given motive, what all of its symbolic meanings are to the person and how it is connected to other motives.

Another line of evidence comes from studies of *changes* in motivation as a result of organizational experience. It has been difficult to determine, for example, whether an alienated worker was a person without achievement and self-actualization needs when he first joined an organization, or whether he became that way as a result of chronically frustrating work experiences. The point is critical, because if motives are not capable of being elicited or stimulated, more emphasis should be placed on *selecting* those workers who initially display the patterns of motivation required by the organization; if, on the other hand, by changing organizational arrangements and managerial strategies, it is possible to arouse the kinds of motives desired, more emphasis should be given to helping *organizations change.*

I have already mentioned the evidence of case studies such as those done in companies which have adopted the Scanlon Plan. Workers who for years took an apathetic attitude toward organizational goals were able, with an organizational change, to become highly motivated and committed to such goals.

In one of the few field studies concerned with changes, Lieberman attempted to determine what *attitude* changes would occur as a result of shifting a man's role from union steward to foreman.[31] Those stewards who were promoted to foremen showed consistent attitude changes—from pro-union to pro-management—within a few months of the promotion. Because of economic reverses, the company had to demote some of these foremen. When their attitudes were studied again, it turned out that they had again adopted the attitudes of the worker group and abandoned their pro-management attitudes.

RECAPITULATION: AUTHORITY, THE PSYCHOLOGICAL CONTRACT, AND THE PROCESS OF MANAGEMENT IN PERSPECTIVE

In this chapter we have examined the relationship of the individual and the organization from various points of view. First, with Etzioni's typology, from the point of view of the basic types of power or authority used by organizations and the basic kinds of involvement people have in organizations. Then we examined the process of management in terms of some of the major sets of assumptions which have been made about man in organizations,

[30] S.W. Gellerman. *Motivation and productivity.* New York: Amer. Management Assoc., 1963.

[31] S. Lieberman. The effects of changes in roles on the attitudes of role occupants. *Human Relations,* 1956, 9, 385–402.

and spelled out the implications of these assumptions for the nature of superior-subordinate authority, the kind of psychological contract which was implied, and the actual managerial strategy which resulted. Insofar as possible, we then reviewed the empirical evidence for each of the sets of assumptions, starting with rational-economic man, going to social man and self-actualizing man, and closing with a more balanced attempt to describe the complexity inherent in man.

The emphasis in this chapter has been on motivation, particularly the motivation of the employee, but motivation is, of course, not the only determinant of effective performance. The ability of the person, the nature of the work setting and the supply of tools and materials, the nature of the job itself, and the ability of management to coordinate the efforts of many— all enter into organizational effectiveness.[32] The reason for our focus on motivation and our extensive exploration of it rests, however, on the fact that in the motivational area there have been more myths and misconceptions than in any of the others. It has been particularly difficult for practitioners to resist the temptation to infer motives from observed organizational behavior. In particular, it has been easy to accept organizational circumstances as a given condition and to explain behavior variations as a function of different motives. Thus, the good worker could be assumed to have a high achievement need while the poor worker or alienated worker could be assumed to lack ambition. In some cases, the assumption would have been correct. But, as I have argued, in other situations, it would have been more correct to see the good worker as having a boss who challenges him while the poor worker has a boss who gives him fragmented and intrinsically meaningless assignments. The motivational potential of the two may in fact be identical.

The number of studies which have shown, both for productivity and for the satisfaction and psychological growth of employees, the superiority of supervisory strategies which involve employee participation in decision-making are now sufficient to suggest strongly that more shared decision-making, greater influence for employees, and power equilization should be seriously considered for many kinds of organizations. They will not work all the time and for all people. But they should be attempted before one concludes that the human resources of the organization are hopeless and must be replaced through selection methods with "better" people.

By way of conclusion, I would like to underline the importance of the psychological contract as a major variable of analysis. It is my central hypothesis that whether a person is working effectively, whether he generates commitment, loyalty, and enthusiasm for the organization and its goals, and whether he obtains satisfaction from his work, depend to a large measure on two conditions: (1) the degree to which his own expectations of what the organization will provide him and what he owes the organization matches

---

[32] For example, in a recent analysis of work and motivation, Vroom has postulated that performance can be hypothesized to be a function of (a) the abilities the person perceives to be required to do the job; (b) the degree to which the person perceives himself to possess those abilities; (c) the degree to which he values the possession of such abilities. Changes in any one or more of these psychological variables can affect both actual performance and satisfaction with the job. V.H. Vroom. *Work and motivation.* New York: Wiley, 1964.

what the organization's expectations are of what it will give and get; (2) assuming there is agreement on expectations, what actually is to be exchanged —money in exchange for time at work; social-need satisfaction and security in exchange for work and loyalty; opportunities for self-actualization and challenging work in exchange for high productivity, quality work, and creative effort in the service of organizational goals; or various combinations of these and other things.

Ultimately the relationship between the individual and the organization is interactive, unfolding through mutual influence and mutual bargaining to establish a workable psychological contract. We cannot understand the psychological dynamics if we look only to the individual's motivations or only to organizational conditions and practices. The two interact in a complex fashion, requiring us to develop theories and research approaches which can deal with systems and interdependent phenomena.[33]

Just as the manner in which a person is selected, trained, and assigned influences his image of the organization, so the manner in which he is managed will influence this image. A manager must be aware of the interaction between these various organizational systems and must think integratively about them. For example, if he plans to manage people in a way which will challenge them and provide them with opportunities to use all their potential, he must be careful that the manner in which they are selected, tested, trained, and assigned to their jobs does not undermine the very motivations he wishes to draw on. What this means in practice is that all those members of the organization who are responsible for the various functions should, together, think through carefully the consequences of the various approaches, and coordinate their activities to accomplish whatever shared goals they have.

[33] In some experimental studies which attempted to test directly the relationship of feelings of equity in the psychological contract to productivity on a task, Adams showed that subjects who feel they are being overpaid for their level of ability will produce more than subjects who feel they are being fairly paid relative to their level of ability. The interpretation is that if the organization gives more than it gets, in the eyes of the subject, he will work harder to make the relationship more just. J.S. Adams and W.B. Rosenbaum. The relationship of worker productivity to cognitive dissonance about wage inequities. *J. appl. Psychol.*, 1962, 46, 161–164.

Groups and Intergroup Relationships

Groups in organizations have become the subject of much mythology and the target for strong feelings. Though groups are nearly universal in organizations, some managers who have little faith in teamwork and committees pride themselves on running an operation in which things are done only by individuals, not by groups. Elsewhere, one finds managers saying with equal pride that they make all their major decisions in groups and rely heavily on teamwork. People differ greatly in their stereotypes of what a group is, what a group can and cannot do, and how effective a group can be. A classic joke told by those who are against the

5

use of groups is that "a camel is a horse which was put together by a committee."

What, then, is the "truth" about groups? Why do they exist? What functions do groups fulfill for the organization and for their members? How should one conceptualize a group, and how does one judge the goodness or effectiveness of a group? What kinds of things can groups do and what can they not do? What impact do groups have on their members, on each other, and on the organization within which they exist? What are the pro's and con's of intergroup cooperation and intergroup competition? How does one manage and influence groups? These are some of the questions we will discuss in this chapter.

The reason for devoting an entire chapter to groups is that there is ample evidence that they do have a major impact on their members, on other groups, and on the host organization. Their existence ultimately is stimulated by the very concept of organization. As I indicated in Chapter 2, an organization divides up its ultimate task into subtasks which are assigned to various subunits. These subunits in turn may divide the task and pass it down further, until a level is reached where several people take a subgoal and divide it among themselves as individuals, but no longer create units. At this level of formal organization, we have the basis for group formation along functional lines. The sales department or some part thereof may come to be a group; the production department may be a single group or a set of groups; and so on. What basically breaks an organization into groups, therefore, is division of labor. The organization itself generates forces toward the formation of various smaller functional task groups within itself.

DEFINITION OF A GROUP

How big is a group and what characterizes it? It has generally been difficult to define a group, independent of some specific purpose or frame of reference. Since we are examining psychological problems in organizations, it would appear most appropriate to define the group in psychological terms.

A psychological group is any number of people who (1) interact with one another, (2) are psychologically aware of one another, and (3) perceive themselves to be a group.

The size of the group is thus limited by the possibilities of mutual interaction and mutual awareness. Mere aggregates of people do not fit this definition because they do not interact and do not perceive themselves to be a group even if they are aware of each other as, for instance, a crowd on a street corner watching some event. A total department, a union, or a whole organization would not be a group in spite of thinking of themselves as "we," because they generally do not all interact and are not all aware of each other. Work teams, committees, subparts of departments, cliques, and various other informal associations among organizational members would fit this definition of a group.

Having defined a group, and having indicated that the basic force toward group formation arises out of the organizational process itself, let us now examine the kinds of groups which are actually found in organizations and the functions which such groups appear to fulfill for the organization and for its members.

Formal Groups

Formal groups are created in order to fulfill specific goals and carry on specific tasks which are clearly related to the total organizational mission. Formal groups can be of two types, based on their duration. *Permanent* formal groups are bodies such as the top management team, work units in the various departments of the organization, staff groups providing specialized services to the work organization, permanent committees, and so on. *Temporary* formal groups are committees or task forces which may be created to carry out a particular job but which, once the job is carried out, cease to exist unless some other task is found for them or unless they take on informal functions. Thus, an organization may create a committee or study group to review salary policies, to study the relationship between the organization and the community, to try to invent some proposals for improving relations between the union and management, to thing of new products and services, and so on. Temporary formal groups may exist for a long time. What makes them temporary is that they are defined as such by the organization and that the members feel themselves to be a part of a group which may at any time go out of existence.

Informal Groups

As I have pointed out, the members of organizations are formally called upon to provide only certain activities to fulfill their organizational role. But, because the whole man actually reports for work or joins the organization and because man has needs beyond the minimum ones of doing his job, he will seek fulfillment of some of these needs through developing a variety of relationships with other members of the organization. If the ecology of the work area and the time schedule of the work permit, these informal relationships will develop into informal groups. In other words, the *tendency* toward informal groups can almost always be assumed to exist because of the nature of man. How this tendency works itself out in the actual creation of groups, however, depends very much on the physical location of people, the nature of their work, their time schedules, and so on. Informal groups therefore arise out of the particular combination of "formal" factors and human needs.

Some examples may help to clarify this important point. It has been found in a number of studies of friendship and informal association that such relationships can be predicted to a large degree simply from the probability of who would meet whom in the day-to-day routine. In a housing project, this likelihood was largely determined by the actual location and direction of doorways.[1] Those people who met because their doorways faced were more likely to become friends than those whose doorways made meeting less likely.

[1] L. Festinger, S. Schachter, and K. Back. *Social pressures in informal groups: a study of a housing project.* New York: Harper, 1950.

In the bank-wiring room of the Hawthorne studies, the two major informal cliques were the "group in the front" and the "group in the back," this pattern arising out of actual job-related interactions as well as slight differences in the work performed in the two parts of the room. The reason why the men in front considered themselves to be superior was that they were doing more difficult work, though they were not actually paid more for it. Thus, informal groups tend to arise partly out of the formal features of the organization.

If the organization sets itself to *prevent* informal group formation, it can do so by designing the work and its physical layout in such a way that no opportunities for interaction arise, as in the case of the assembly line, or it can systematically rotate leaders and key members to prevent any stable group structure from emerging, as the Chinese Communists did in handling American prisoners of war in Korea.[2]

Assuming that the organization does not set out to limit informal group formation, and that the nature of the work permits it, what kinds of informal groups do we find in organizations? The commonest kinds can be called, to follow Dalton's terminology, *horizontal cliques*.[3] By this, he means an informal association of workers, managers, or organizational members who are more or less of the same rank, and work in more or less the same area. The bank-wiring room had two such cliques in it. Most organizations which have been studied, regardless of their basic function (that is, mutual benefit, business, commonweal, or service), have an extensive informal organization consisting of many such cliques.

A second type, which can be called a *vertical clique,* is a group composed of members from different levels within a given department. For example, in several organizations which Dalton studied, he found groups which consisted of a number of workers, one or two foremen, and one or more higher-level managers. Some of the members were actually in superior-subordinate relationships to one another. A group such as this apparently comes into being because of earlier acquaintance of the members or because they need each other to accomplish their goals. For example, such groups often serve a key communication function both upward and downward.

A third type of clique can be called a *mixed clique*.[4] This will have in it members of different ranks, from different departments, and from different physical locations. Such cliques may arise to serve common interests or to fulfill functional needs which are not taken care of by the organization (for example, the head of manufacturing may cultivate a relationship with the best worker in the maintenance department in order to be able to short-circuit formal communication channels when a machine breaks down and he needs immediate maintenance work). Relationships outside of the organizational context may be an important basis for the formation of such cliques. For example, a number of members may live in the same part of town, or attend the same church, or belong to the same social club. These outside associations may be transferred to the organization.

[2] E.H. Schein. The Chinese indoctrination program for prisoners of war. *Psychiatry,* 1956, 19, 149–172.

[3] M. Dalton. *Men who manage.* New York: Wiley, 1959.

[4] Dalton has called these "random" cliques.

Formal, Organizational Functions

By formal, organizational functions, I mean those which pertain to the accomplishment of the organization's basic mission. Thus, by definition, formal groups serve certain formal functions such as getting work out, generating ideas, or serving as liaison. The formal functions are the tasks which are assigned to the group and for which it is officially held responsible.

Psychological, Personal Functions

Because organizational members bring with them a variety of needs, and because group formation can fulfill many of these needs, we can list a number of psychological functions which groups fulfill for their members. Groups can provide:

a. An outlet for *affiliation needs,* that is, needs for friendship, support, and love.

b. A means of *developing, enhancing, or confirming a sense of identity and maintaining self-esteem.* Through group membership a person can develop or confirm some feelings of who he is, can gain some status, and thereby enhance his sense of self-esteem.

c. A means of *establishing and testing reality.* Through developing consensus among group members, uncertain parts of the social environment can be made "real" and stable, as when several workers agree that their boss is a slave-driver or when by mutual agreement they establish the reality that if they work harder, management will cut the piece rate of whatever they are making. Each person can validate his own perceptions and feelings best by checking them with others.

d. A means of *increasing security and a sense of power* in coping with a common and powerful enemy or threat. Through banding together into bargaining units such as unions or through agreeing to restrict output, groups can offset some of the power which management has over members individually.

e. A means of *getting some job done which members need to have done,* such as gathering information, or helping out when some are sick or tired, or avoiding boredom and providing stimulation to one another, or bringing new members of the organization quickly into the informal structure, and so on.

Multiple or Mixed Functions

One of the commonest findings which comes from the study of groups in organizations—and which, incidentally, is a reason why organizations are so much more complex than traditional organization theory envisioned—is that most groups turn out to have both formal and informal functions; they serve the needs of both the organization and the individual members. Psychological groups, therefore, may well be the key unit for facilitating the integration of organizational goals and personal needs.

Groups
and Intergroup
Relationships

For example, a formal work crew such as is found in industry or in the Army (say, a platoon) often becomes a psychological group which meets a variety of the psychological needs mentioned. If this process occurs, it often becomes the source of much higher levels of loyalty, commitment, and energy in the service of organizational goals than would be possible if the psychological needs were met in informal groups which did not coincide with the formal one. One key issue for research and for management practice, therefore, is the determination of the conditions which will facilitate the fulfillment of psychological needs in *formal* work groups.

An example of an informal group which begins to serve formal, organizational functions would be the kind of grouping, found by Dalton, which enables top management to use informal channels of communication to obtain information quickly on conditions in various parts of the organization, and which also enables line operators to determine quickly what changes in production policy are in the offing and prepare them long before they are formally announced. The actual mechanism might be the exchange of information at lunch, at the local meeting of the Rotary Club, over golf at the country club, or through an informal telephone conversation. According to Dalton, these contacts not only meet many psychological needs, but they are clearly *necessary* for the maintenance of organizational effectiveness.

In such groups, we again find an integration of formal organizational needs with informal psychological needs. The problem here, also, is to discover the conditions which will make such groups use their informal resources for the fulfillment of organizational goals rather than band together to defeat organizational goals or become competitive with one another and thereby undermine organizational integration.

VARIABLES AFFECTING THE INTEGRATION IN GROUPS OF ORGANIZATIONAL GOALS AND PERSONAL NEEDS

There are a variety of factors that will determine the kinds of groups which will tend to exist in an organization and whether such groups will tend to fulfill both organizational and personal functions or only one or the other. These variables can be divided up into three classes: environmental factors—the cultural, social, and technological climate in which the group exists; membership factors—the kinds of people, categorized in terms of personal background, values, relative status, and so on, who are in the group; and dynamic factors—how the group is organized, the manner in which the group is led or managed, the amount of training members have received in leadership and membership skills, the kinds of tasks given to the group, its prior history of success or failure, and so on.

Environmental Factors

Environmental factors such as the organization of the work, the physical location of workers, and the time schedule imposed will determine who will interact with whom and therefore which people are likely to form into groups in the first place. If groups are to be encouraged to fulfill organizational tasks, it obviously follows that the work environment must permit and, in fact, promote the emergence of "logical" groups. This end can be accomplished by actually designating certain groups as work teams, or allowing groups to emerge by facilitating interaction and allowing enough free time for it to occur.

In many cases, the nature or location of a job itself requires effective group action, as in bomber, tank, or submarine crews, in groups who work in isolation for long periods of time (say, in a radar station), or in medical teams or ward personnel in a hospital. In other cases, even though the technical requirements do not demand it, an organization often encourages group formation. For example, the Army, rather than replace soldiers one at a time, has begun to use four-man groups who go through basic training together as combat replacements. In the hotel industry, where it is crucial that the top management of a given hotel work well together, one chain has begun a conscious program of training the top team together before they take charge of a hotel in order to insure good working relations.

The degree to which such logically designed groups come to serve psychological needs will depend to a large extent on another environmental factor —the managerial climate. The managerial climate is determined primarily by the prevailing assumptions in the organization about the nature of man. If assumptions of *rational-economic man* are favored, it is unlikely that groups will be rationally utilized in the first place. According to those assumptions, groups are at most to be tolerated or, preferably, destroyed in the interest of maximizing individual efficiency. If coordination is required, it is to be supplied by the assembly line or some other mechanical means.

Consequently, it is in a climate built on assumptions of rational-economic man that defensive antimanagement informal groups are most likely to arise. One of the primary psychological functions is to enable members to feel more secure and to gain power for use against management. A secondary function is to obtain status and self-esteem, but, in this case also, status and self-esteem which the formal organization denies the worker through the demeaning nature of the work itself.

An organization built on the assumptions and values of *social man* will encourage and foster the growth of groups, but may err in not being logical in creating groupings which will facilitate task performance. This kind of organization often maintains a philosophy of job design and job allocation built on the assumptions of rational-economic man, but then attempts to meet man's affiliative needs by creating various social groups for him *extrinsic* to the immediate work organization—company bowling leagues, baseball teams, picnics, and social activities. The organizational logic then dictates that in exchange for the fulfillment of his social needs, a man should work harder on his individually designed job. This logic does not permit the integration of formal and informal group forces, because the groups have no intrinsic *task* function in the first place.

An organization built on the assumptions and values of *self-actualizing man* is more likely to create a climate conducive to the emergence of psychologically meaningful groups because of the organization's concern with the meaningfulness of work. However, such organizations—for example, research divisions of industrial concerns or university departments—often fail to see the importance of groups as a means for individual self-actualization. So much emphasis is given to challenging each individual and so little emphasis is given to collective effort in which individual contributions are difficult to judge, that groups are not likely to be encouraged or allowed to develop.

The effective integration of organizational and personal needs probably requires a climate based on the assumptions of *complex man* because groups are not the right answer to all problems at all times. Those organizations which are able to use groups effectively tend to be very careful in deciding when to make use of a work team or a committee and when to set up conditions which promote or discourage group formation. There are no easy generalizations in this area, hence a diagnostic approach may be the most likely to pay off. The type of task involved, the past history of the organization with regard to the use of groups, the people available and their ability to be effective group members, the kind of group leadership available—these are all critical.

Membership Factors

Whether a group will work effectively on an organizational task and at the same time become psychologically satisfying to its members depends in part on the group composition. For any effective work to occur, there must be a certain amount of *consensus on basic values and on a medium of communication.* If personal backgrounds, values, or status differentials prevent communication, the group cannot perform well. It is particularly important that relative status be carefully assessed in order to avoid the fairly common situation where a lower-ranking member will not give accurate information to a higher-ranking member because he does not wish to be punished for saying possibly unpleasant things or things he believes the other does not wish to hear.

The commonest example is the departmental staff meeting in which the boss asks his various subordinates how things are going in their units. In the typical situation, subordinates will respond only with vague statements that everything is all right because they know that the boss wants and expects things that way, and because they do not wish to be embarrassed in front of their peers by admitting failures. Consequently, for problem-solving, such a group is very ineffective.

Another typically difficult group is a committee composed of representatives of various departments of the organization. Each person is likely to be so concerned about the group he came from, wishing to uphold its interests as its representative, that it becomes difficult for the members to become identified with the new committee.

A third kind of problem group, illustrating conflict of values, is the typical labor-management bargaining committee. Even though the mission of the group may be to invent new solutions to chronic problems, the labor members typically cannot even establish good communications with the management members because they feel that the latter look down upon them, devalue them as human beings, and do not respect them. These attitudes may be communicated in subtle ways, such as by asking that the meetings be held in management's meeting rooms rather than offering to meet on neutral territory or in a place suggested by the labor group.

An inadequate distribution of relevant abilities and skills may be another important membership problem. For any work group to be effective, it must have within it the resources to fulfill the task it is given. If the group fails in accomplishing its task because of lack of resources and thereby develops a psychological sense of failure, it can hardly develop the strength and cohesiveness to serve other psychological needs for its members. All of these points indicate that just bringing a collection of people into interaction does not insure a good working group. It is important to consider the characteristics of the members and to assess the likelihood of their being able to work with one another and serve one another's needs.[5]

Dynamic Factors

By dynamic factors, I mean those events and processes which occur during the life of the group itself or which lead up to the formation of the group, such as training people to become a group or inducing certain group feelings. In this category would be variables like the manner in which members are oriented to and brought into the group, the kind of group structure which emerges out of the actual interactions of the members (as contrasted with the imposed structure), the success and failure the group has in reference both to fulfilling its formal task (if it is a formal group) and to meeting the psychological needs of its members.

Dynamic factors highlight the changing and changeable nature of groups. Groups are not static, rigid, or unchangeable. In fact, one of the major contributions of the field of group dynamics has been a body of knowledge and a related body of skills concerned with actually helping groups to change, grow, and become more effective. Instead of taking environmental and membership factors as fixed, imposing rigid limits on what a group can and cannot do, we have discovered that such factors can provide opportunities for group growth and can, if properly utilized, be turned into advantages rather than disadvantages.

Entire texts have been written just on the psychology of groups and how to work with them.[6] I will not be able to review even a small portion of the large amount of information available, but would like to give some illustrations and draw attention to some of the key variables and key issues which are involved. Let us start with a case example.

The Oil Refinery Labor-Management Conflict. A large oil refinery was having difficulty in its labor-management relations, and was threatened with having many of its employees vote to join a rather hostile and militant union. Several committees had been set up to find new solutions to the many problems brought up by the employees, but these committees invariably broke down in an antagonistic deadlock after a few meetings, with both labor and management members feeling that the other side was stubborn and recalcitrant.

[5] A number of research studies have attempted to determine whether group effectiveness could be predicted from personality variables. Among these the best example is William Schutz' work reported in *FIRO: A three-dimensional theory of interpersonal behavior*. New York: Holt, Rinehart, and Winston, 1958.

[6] One of the best books of this nature is M. Miles. *Learning to work in groups*. New York: Bureau of Publications, Teachers College, Columbia Univ., 1959.

Thus far, the story is fairly typical of many labor-management conflicts. However, this particular refinery had instituted a training program devoted specifically to helping trainees become more familiar with problems of being an effective group leader and group member and with obtaining some insight into their own behavior in groups and their impact on other people. The program involved two weeks of full-time training in interpersonal relations and group dynamics and resulted in considerable attitude change and personal insight for the trainees. The plan was eventually to have all members of management and the professional staff services, like research and engineering, attend the two-week program; but long before this goal had been accomplished, the labor crisis reached new proportions.

Management at this point decided to try still one more set of problem-solving committees, but this time, having gained some insight into group functioning, composed them and launched them in a very different manner. First of all, only management members who had been through the training program, and who were therefore assumed to be more sensitive to group problems, were put on the committees. Secondly, the groups were instructed not to arrive at decisions (in previous efforts the drive toward decisions had resulted in premature polarization of opinions) but to explore certain of the issues with the aim of identifying alternatives. Thirdly, the management members were carefully instructed to allow the initiative for meeting times, locations, and agenda details to remain with the labor members.

From the outset, these committees had a very different kind of climate. They were oriented far more toward problem-solving than toward worrying about which member had how much status; and indeed, they generated proposals which led to an overwhelming defeat of the militant union's effort to organize the refinery. Although it is difficult in such a case to identify the exact cause-and-effect relationships, there is little question that major ameliorating forces were the training some members had received in being an effective group member and the greater insight management had as a result of the training in how to compose and launch groups.

Training for Effective Group Membership and Leadership through Laboratory Methods.   One major determinant of group effectiveness is the sensitivity of group members and formal leaders to the kinds of problems which groups generate. Members failing to pay attention to each other and thus communicating, whether intentionally or not, a lack of respect for one another; members being preoccupied with their own emotional needs for status, security, attention, influence, and comfort, leading to failure to listen to others; leaders failing to sense either of the above problems and speeding the group into performance before it is psychologically prepared to pay attention to a group task; leaders prematurely polarizing opinion by early use of parliamentary procedures which often lead to voting among already available alternatives before some of the more creative and *new* alternatives have had an opportunity to be invented; leaders or members being insensitive to status differentials within the group which, unless resolved, block communication; leaders or members failing to note and evaluate group norms and pressures toward conformity which build up around such norms: These and many other kinds of problems are chronic in most groups, although members are unaware of them and therefore cannot do anything about them. Yet the growth and effectiveness of the group depend on understanding such problems and coping with them rationally.

One approach which has had considerable success in helping groups to become more effective is the *laboratory method of training or re-education.*[7] The essential assumptions underlying this form of training are (1) that people can learn best from an analysis of their own immediate "here-and-now" psychological experiences; (2) that the relevant facts from which such learning can best arise are the feelings, reactions, and observations of other people with whom they interact, *which they for a variety of reasons systematically withhold from each other;* (3) that a suitably designed training laboratory can overcome the forces against sharing feelings, reactions, and observations and thus make available to participants learning at this more immediate and potent level; and (4) that the forces to be overcome are essentially culturally learned attitudes about the proper things people should say to one another and attitudes about how one learns (for instance, "one should not deliberately say something critical to another person," and "the way one learns is by listening to and reading the writings of an expert").

The lab method challenges and successfully changes some of these attitudes, making it possible for participants to obtain personal insight into their own as well as others' reactions and feelings about the commonly shared and observed group events.

Many kinds of concrete training devices are used to facilitate this kind of learning, ranging from role-playing, followed by an analysis of each role-player's performance, to unstructured sensitivity-training groups in which members experience the process of building a group literally from the beginning and analyze the process as they are going through it.[8] For example, such a group may discover early in its history (after some three to six hours of meeting) (1) that it is having great difficulty obtaining agreement on a topic to discuss, and (2) that members actually do not listen to each other or pay much attention to each other. An important insight, then, may be that personal concerns (each member's preoccupation with his own needs) are at first much greater than concern for others or for total group performance, and that the difficulty of making a decision on the topic is thereby easily explainable.

Having had this experience in the laboratory, the participant often discovers that analogous events are occurring in the work groups and committees in his organization, but that no one is aware of them and therefore cannot work on them. Yet, once the problem is identified, even such a simple thing as giving the committee enough time to allow members to feel each other out and find a secure place for themselves in the group (which may take no more than an hour or two of low-pressure informal talk), may make it possible thereafter for the group to work effectively on a high-pressure problem. It is

[7] For a detailed description of this type of training, refer to E.H. Schein, and W.G. Bennis. *Personal and organizational change through group methods.* New York: Wiley, 1965.

[8] Such groups have generally been called T-groups (training) and have been widely used in human relations training. Further analysis of how and why such groups produce powerful learning experiences can be found in L.P. Bradford, J.R. Gibb, and K.D. Benne (eds.). *T-group theory and laboratory method.* New York: Wiley, 1964. Also in E.H. Schein and W.G. Bennis. *Op. cit.*

this kind of insight which was generated by the refinery's training program and which made it possible for the management members to create a better climate for problem-solving in the newly created labor-management committees.

One question which always arises in reference to laboratory training concerns the content of what is learned. For example, does this form of training attempt to teach democratic leadership methods, and does it undermine the traditional prerogatives of authority positions, leading ultimately to greater "power-equalization"? If so, does this not undermine many organizational settings, as in the military, or in industry, where authority must be upheld and must continue to be highly centralized?

The answers to these questions are complex. The ultimate values that are communicated through laboratory training are (1) an increased commitment to a spirit of inquiry and a diagnostic approach to interpersonal and organizational situations, both of which are essentially the values of science, and (2) a commitment to the value of open and honest communication wherever appropriate. In terms of the spirit of inquiry, it may well be that the important insight coming out of training is that a group should be run autocratically in order to achieve its goals. If that conclusion is based on a careful assessment of all factors, it is completely valid and not inconsistent with the philosophy of laboratory training. But a commitment to open sharing of feelings and reactions does inevitably imply some democratization. The effective exercise of formal authority, in contrast, implies a *limiting of communicaton* to task-relevant information and a systematic *exclusion of feelings* in the interests of efficiency. To teach people the value of being more open and honest, then, does undermine formal authority to a considerable degree. The important point to bear in mind, however, is that, to judge from mounting research evidence, in many situations where formal authority has been assumed to be necessary, it proves to be not only *un*necessary but also inefficient, by creating a variety of human problems which undermine task performance. As most of the research cited in Chapter 4 showed, formal systems of authority tend to be based on an unrealistic model of man and therefore to foster hostile, antiorganization informal groups.

The resolution of the issue lies in being sufficiently aware of the important organizational factors at work to know when it is and is not appropriate to be open and honest. And this kind of awareness, paradoxically, can develop best from a kind of training which teaches both a spirit of inquiry and the value of openness and requires a certain amount of openness during the training period itself in order for participants to learn either of the above values.

In summary, a major factor leading to group effectiveness, either in doing the job or in meeting members' psychological needs, is the sensitivity and skill of members and leaders in diagnosing and working on group problems. Such sensitivity and skill can best be obtained in a laboratory setting where the participant learns from an analysis of his own experiences and feelings in group situations. Such training can improve group effectiveness, but care must be taken to insure that the values and assumptions of laboratory training are compatible with the values and assumptions of the organization, since training of this sort intervenes in the ongoing organizational system.

Group History and Tradition.   If there is a change in group leadership, the new leader often finds that he cannot impose his particular conception of how the group should operate unless he adapts to the major norms and traditions of the group. If he persists, he may either reduce the effectiveness of the group or undermine its existence. A common pitfall is for a manager with a newly found democratic theory of leadership to attempt to practice it on a work group whose history and traditions have been autocratic. What may well happen is that the group will perform more poorly under a style it is not used to, which in turn may lead the manager to the erroneous conclusion that the democratic style does not work. It may be just as hard for a group to shift from autocratic leadership as it is to shift from democratic to autocratic.

Group Organizational patterns.   If the group cannot meet face-to-face at all times, it becomes important to consider the existing communications network and its consequences for group functioning. For example, it has been shown that a person's feeling of participation is related to his position in a communications network; that group leadership may well emerge from the more central positions; that overcentralized communications are very effective in implementing a given task but relatively inflexible in developing new solutions if the task changes; that information is lost and distorted very rapidly as it travels through a number of separate communication links.[9]

Leaders' Perceptions of Group Members.   In an extensive series of studies of different kinds of task groups, Fiedler has consistently been able to show that an effective group, whether a basketball team, tank crew, or business group, is characterized by a particular relationship between leader and follower.[10] Fiedler found that the accepted leader of an effective group tends to perceive greater differences between what he considers his best and worst group member than does the accepted leader of a less effective group. In other words, one characteristic of an effective group is that the accepted leader perceives greater differences among his members. (This is not the case if the formal leader of the group is not accepted by the members. In this instance, how he perceives group members does not correlate with group effectiveness.) It is not clear whether the leader of the effective group is more likely to reject his worst workers while the leader of the less effective group continues to accept them, or whether it simply reflects the former's more accurate perception of reality, enabling him to use his resources more appropriately.

"Task" and "Socio-Emotional" Leadership.   The distinction I have been making between formal functions of accomplishing a task and psychological functions of fulfilling members' emotional needs has been studied in artificial groups in the laboratory. It has been shown that most groups have to fulfill both sets of functions to some degree and that leadership consists of behavior which helps the group to achieve one or the other. Some social psychologists

[9] For examples of this type of research, see H.J. Leavitt. Some effects of certain communication patterns on group performance. *J. abnorm. soc. Psychol.*, 1951, 46, 38–50.

[10] F.E. Fiedler. *Leader attitudes and group effectiveness.* Urbana: Univ. of Illinois Press, 1958.

have labelled these as "task" and "socio-emotional" behavior. Bales has developed a system for rating individual behavior and classifying it by function in either category.[11]

Studying many groups doing a variety of tasks, he has found that the leader who emerges as the "task" leader is not necessarily the same person who emerges as the "socio-emotional" leader. In fact, the two roles generally tend to be taken by different persons. It would be interesting to determine whether organizational groups which develop their own informal leaders do so because the formal leader is somehow failing to help the group members fulfill their socio-emotional needs.

When to Use a Group—Group vs. Individual Performance. A great deal of research has been devoted to the question of whether the group or isolated individuals whose work can be pooled is the more effective problem-solving instrument. No definitive answer has yet been reached, but some key variables have been identified and some myths have been exploded. For example, it has been believed that group decisions on problems involving an element of risk would be more conservative than individual decisions on those same problems. Research by Marquis, Wallach, and others [12] has shown that often exactly the opposite trend occurs.

It is widely believed that groups are very slow and inefficient, yet case evidence has shown that if a group is composed of members who trust one another and have learned to work well together, it can work more quickly and efficiently than any member alone because it can more rapidly gather and process the information necessary for a decision. It is true, however, that if the group has not achieved mutual trust and confidence, it will be slower and less efficient than an individual.

It has been believed that a group can be more creative than individuals because of the mutual stimulation members can provide to one another, but this proves to be true only under certain circumstances—such as having a nonevaluative climate in the group, a decision-making structure appropriate to the task, and enough time to explore the unusual idea—and on certain kinds of tasks [13]—such as those that involve the gathering of a wide range of information or that require a complex evaluation of the consequences of various alternatives. In a group setting, errors of judgment are more likely to be identified before action is taken than if the individual is attempting to think through all the alternatives himself.

One of the most important criteria for determining whether to use a group in making a decision involves an assessment of why and how the decision is to be implemented. People are more likely to carry out a decision that they have

[11] R.F. Bales. Task roles and social roles in problem-solving groups. In Eleanor E. Maccoby, T.M. Newcomb, and E.L. Hartley (eds.). *Readings in social psychology.* 3rd ed. New York: Holt, Rinehart, and Winston, 1958.

[12] M.A. Wallach, N. Kogan, and D.J. Bem. Group influence on individual risk taking. *J. abnorm. soc. Psychol.,* 1962, 65, 75–86. Also D.G. Marquis. Individual responsibility and group decisions involving risk. *Ind. Mgt. Rev.,* 1962, 3, 8–23.

[13] D.W. Taylor, P.C. Berry, and C.H. Block. Does group participation when using brainstorming facilitate or inhibit creative thinking? *Admin. Science Quart.,* 1958, 3, 23–47.

had a hand in making than one that has been imposed. If effective implementation is critical, therefore, it is important to involve the implementers as much as possible, if only by asking them whether they see any problems with a proposed decision.

If a group is used to perform a task, it is critical that the leader recognize and understand some of the many dynamic, environmental, and membership factors which have been discussed in the above pages. If he does, he will allow the group to develop and mature into an effective unit before expecting high-level performance. But if he ignores these factors, he may well land in the trap of expecting people who have been called together to be able automatically to perform as an effective psychological group. If they fail to perform, he may then erroneously conclude that groups are ineffective. What he does not realize is that, in a sense, he did not have a group in the first place, only an aggregate of people. One of the major contributions of laboratory training to group dynamics has been to make people sensitive to the complexity of groups and to the time and energy which must be invested early in order to obtain effective performance later.

INTERGROUP PROBLEMS IN ORGANIZATIONS

The first major problem of groups in organizations is how to make them effective in fulfilling both organizational goals and the needs of their members. The second major problem is how to establish conditions *between groups* which will enhance the productivity of each without destroying intergroup relations and coordination. This problem exists because as groups become more committed to their own goals and norms, they are likely to become competitive with one another and seek to undermine their rivals' activities, thereby becoming a liability to the organization as a whole. The over-all problem, then, is how to establish high-productive, *collaborative* intergroup relations.

Some Consequences of Intergroup Competition

The consequences of intergroup competition were first studied systematically by Sherif in an ingeniously designed setting. He organized a boys' camp in such a way that two groups would form and would become competitive. Sherif then studied the effects of the competition and tried various devices for re-establishing collaborative relationships between the groups.[14] Since his original experiments, there have been many replications with adult groups; the phenomena are so constant that it has been possible to make a demonstration exercise out of the experiment.[15] The effects can be described in terms of the following categories:

[14] M. Sherif, O.J. Harvey, B.J. White, W.R. Hood, and Carolyn Sherif. *Intergroup conflict and cooperation: the robbers cave experiment.* Norman, Okla.: Univ. Book Exchange, 1961.
[15] R.R. Blake and Jane S. Mouton. Reactions to intergroup competition under win-lose conditions. *Management Science,* 1961, 7, 420–435.

A. What happens *within* each competing group?
1. Each group becomes more closely knit and elicits greater loyalty from its members; members close ranks and bury some of their internal differences.
2. Group climate changes from informal, casual, playful to work- and task-oriented; concern for members' psychological needs declines while concern for task accomplishment increases.
3. Leadership patterns tend to change from more democratic toward more autocratic; the group becomes more willing to tolerate autocratic leadership.
4. Each group becomes more highly structured and organized.
5. Each group demands more loyalty and conformity from its members in order to be able to present a "solid front."
B. What happens *between* the competing groups?
1. Each group begins to see the other groups as the enemy, rather than merely a neutral object.
2. Each group begins to experience distortions of perception—it tends to perceive only the best parts of itself, denying its weaknesses, and tends to perceive only the worst parts of the other group, denying its strengths; each group is likely to develop a negative stereotype of the other ("they don't play fair like we do").
3. Hostility toward the other group increases while interaction and communication with the other group decrease; thus it becomes easier to maintain negative stereotypes and more difficult to correct perceptual distortions.
4. If the groups are forced into interaction—for example, if they are forced to listen to representatives plead their own and the others' cause in reference to some task—each group is likely to listen more closely to their own representative and not to listen to the representative of the other group, except to find fault with his presentation; in other words, group members tend to listen only for that which supports their own position and stereotype.

Thus far, I have listed some consequences of the competition itself, without reference to the consequences if one group actually wins out over the other. Before listing those effects, I would like to draw attention to the generality of the above reactions. Whether one is talking about sports teams, or interfraternity competition, or labor-management disputes, or interdepartmental competition as between sales and production in an industrial organization, or about international relations and the competition between the Soviet Union and the United States, the same phenomena tend to occur. If you will give just a little thought to competing groups of which you have been a member, you will begin to recognize most of the psychological responses described. I want to stress that these responses can be very useful to the group in making it more effective and highly motivated in task accomplishment. However, the same factors which improve *intra*group effectiveness may have negative consequences for *inter*group effectiveness. For example, as we have seen in labor-management or international disputes, if the groups perceive themselves as competitors, they find it more difficult to resolve their differences.

Let us next look at the consequences of winning and losing, as in a situation where several groups are bidding to have their proposal accepted for a contract or as a solution to some problem, or in a labor-management negotiation being decided by an arbitrator, or in the typical athletic contest. Many intra-organizational situations become win-or-lose affairs, hence it is of particular importance to examine their consequences.

C. What happens to the *winner*?
1. Winner retains its cohesion and may become even more cohesive.
2. Winner tends to release tension, lose its fighting spirit, become complacent, casual, and playful (the "fat and happy" state).
3. Winner tends toward high intragroup cooperation and concern for members' needs, and low concern for work and task accomplishment.
4. Winner tends to be complacent and to feel that winning has confirmed the positive stereotype of itself and the negative stereotype of the "enemy" group; there is little basis for re-evaluating perceptions, or re-examining group operations in order to learn how to improve them.

D. What happens to the *loser*?
1. If the situation permits because of some ambiguity in the decision (say, if judges have rendered it or if the game was close), there is a strong tendency for the loser to deny or distort the reality of losing; instead, the loser will find psychological escapes like "the judges were biased," "the judges didn't really understand our solution," "the rules of the game were not clearly explained to us," "if luck had not been against us at the one key point, we would have won," and so on.
2. If loss is accepted, the losing group tends to splinter, unresolved conflicts come to the surface, fights break out, all in the effort to find a cause for the loss.
3. Loser is more tense, ready to work harder, and desperate to find someone or something to blame—the leader, itself, the judges who decided against them, the rules of the game (the "lean and hungry" state).
4. Loser tends toward low intragroup cooperation, low concern for members' needs, and high concern for recouping by working harder.
5. Loser tends to learn a lot about itself as a group because positive stereotype of itself and negative stereotype of the other group are upset by the loss, forcing a re-evaluation of perceptions; as a consequence, loser is likely to reorganize and become more cohesive and effective, once the loss has been accepted realistically.

The net effect of the win-lose situation is often that the loser is not convinced that he lost, and that intergroup tension is higher than before the competition began.

The gains of intergroup competition may under some conditions outweigh the negative consequences. It may be desirable to have work groups pitted against one another or to have departments become cohesive loyal units, even if interdepartmental coordination suffers. Other times, however, the negative consequences outweigh the gains, and management seeks ways of reducing intergroup tension. Many of the ideas to be mentioned about how this might be accomplished also come from the basic researches of Sherif and Blake; they have been tested and found to be successful. As we will see, the problems derive not so much from being unable to think of ways for reducing intergroup conflict as from being *unable to implement some of the most effective ways.*

The fundamental problem of intergroup competition is the conflict of goals and the breakdown of interaction and communication between the groups; this breakdown in turn permits and stimulates perceptual distortion and mutual negative stereotyping. The basic strategy of reducing conflict, therefore, is to find goals upon which groups can agree and to re-establish valid communication between the groups. The tactics to employ in implementing this strategy can be any combination of the following:

Locating a common enemy. For example, the competing teams of each league can compose an all-star team to play the other league, or conflicts between sales and production can be reduced if both can harness their efforts to helping their company successfully compete against another company. The conflict here is merely shifted to a higher level.

Inventing a negotiation strategy which brings subgroups of the competing groups into interaction with each other. The isolated group representative cannot abandon his group position but a subgroup which is given some power can not only permit itself to be influenced by its counterpart negotiation team, but will have the strength to influence the remainder of the group.

Locating a superordinate goal. Such a goal can be a brand-new task which requires the cooperative effort of the previously competing groups or can be a task like analyzing and reducing the intergroup conflict itself. For example, the previously competing sales and production departments can be given the task of developing a new product line which will be both cheap to produce and in great customer demand; or, with the help of an outside consultant, the competing groups can be invited to examine their own behavior and re-evaluate the gains and losses from competition.

Reducing Intergroup Competition through Laboratory Training Methods.
The last procedure mentioned above has been tried by a number of psychologists, notably Blake, with considerable success.[16] Assuming the organization recognizes that it has a problem, and assuming it is ready to expose this

---

[16] R.R. Blake, and Jane S. Mouton. Headquarters—field team training for organizational improvement. *J. of the Amer. Soc. of Training Directors,* 1962, 16.

problem to an outside consultant, the laboratory approach to reducing conflict might proceed as follows: (1) The competing groups are both brought into a training setting and the goals are stated to be an exploration of mutual perceptions and mutual relations. (2) Each group is then invited to discuss its perceptions of and attitudes toward itself and the other group. (3) In the presence of both groups, representatives publicly share the perceptions of self and other which the groups have generated, while the groups are obligated to remain silent (the objective is simply to report to the other group as accurately as possible the images that each group has developed in private). (4) Before any exchange has taken place, the groups return to private sessions to digest and analyze what they have heard; there is a great likelihood that the representative reports have revealed great discrepancies to each group between its self-image and the image that the other group holds of it; the private session is partly devoted to an analysis of the reasons for the discrepancies, which forces each group to review its actual behavior toward the other group and the possible consequences of that behavior, regardless of its intentions. (5) In public session, again working through representatives, each group shares with the other what discrepancies they have uncovered and their analysis of the possible reasons for them, with the focus on the actual behavior exhibited. (6) Following this mutual exposure, a more open exploration is then permitted between the two groups on the *now-shared goal* of identifying further reasons for perceptual distortions.

Interspersed with these steps will be short lectures and reading assignments on the psychology of intergroup conflict, the bases for perceptual distortion, psychological defense-mechanisms, and so on. The goal is to bring the psychological dynamics of the situation into conscious awareness and to refocus the groups on the common goal of exploring jointly the problem they share. In order to do this, they must have valid data about each other, which is provided through the artifice of the representative reports.

The Blake model described above deals with the entire group. Various other approaches have been tried which start with members. For example, groups A and B can be divided into pairs composed of an A and B member. Each pair can be given the assignment of developing a joint product which uses the best ideas from the A product and the B product. Or, in each pair, members may be asked to argue for the product of the opposing group. It has been shown in a number of experiments that one way of changing attitudes is to ask a person to play the role of an advocate of the new attitude to be learned.[17] The very act of arguing for another product, even if it is purely an exercise, exposes the person to some of its virtues which he had previously denied. A practical application of these points might be to have some members of the sales department spend some time in the production department and be asked to represent the production point of view to some third party, or to have some production people join sales teams to learn the sales point of view.

Most of the approaches cited depend on a recognition of some problem by

17 I.L. Janis and B.T. King. The influence of role playing on opinion change. *J. abnorm. soc. Psychol.*, 1954, 69, 211–218.

the organization and a willingness on the part of the competing groups to participate in some training effort to reduce negative consequences. The reality, however, is that most organizations neither recognize the problem nor are willing to invest time and energy in resolving it. Some of the unwillingness also arises from each competing group's recognition that in becoming more cooperative it may lose some of its own identity and integrity as a group. Rather than risk this, the group may prefer to continue the competition. This may well be the reason why, in international relations, nations refuse to engage in what seem like perfectly simple ways of resolving their differences. They resist partly in order to protect their integrity. Consequently, the *implementation* of strategies and tactics for reducing the negative consequences of intergroup competition is often a greater problem than the development of such strategies and tactics.

Preventing Intergroup Conflict

Because of the great difficulties of reducing intergroup conflict once it has developed, it may be desirable to prevent its occurrence in the first place. How can this be done? Paradoxically, a strategy of prevention must bring into question the fundamental premise upon which organization through division of labor rests. Once it has been decided by a superordinate authority to divide up functions among different departments or groups, a bias has already been introduced toward intergroup competition; for in doing its own job well, each group must to some degree compete for scarce resources and rewards from the superordinate authority. The very concept of division of labor implies a reduction of communication and interaction between groups, thus making it possible for perceptual distortions to occur.

The organization planner who wishes to avoid intergroup competition need not abandon the concept of division of labor, but he should follow some of the steps listed below in creating and handling his different functional groups.

1. Relatively greater emphasis given to *total organizational effectiveness* and the role of departments in contributing to it; departments measured and rewarded on the basis of their *contribution* to the total effort rather than their individual effectiveness.

2. *High interaction* and *frequent communication* stimulated between groups to work on problems of intergroup coordination and help; organizational *rewards given partly on the basis of help* which groups give to each other.

3. Frequent *rotation of members* among groups or departments to stimulate high degree of mutual understanding and empathy for one anothers' problems.

4. *Avoidance of any win-lose situation;* groups never put into the position of competing for some organizational reward; emphasis always placed on pooling resources to maximize organizational effectiveness; rewards shared equally with all the groups or departments.

Most managers find the last of the above points particularly difficult to accept because of the strong belief that performance can be improved by pitting people or groups against one another in a competitive situation. This may indeed be true in the short run, and in some cases may work in the long run, but the negative consequences we have described are undeniably a product of a competitive win-lose situation. Consequently, if a manager wishes to prevent such consequences, he must face the possibility that he may have to abandon competitive relationships altogether and seek to substitute intergroup collaboration toward organizational goals. Implementing such a preventive strategy is often more difficult, partly because most people are inexperienced in stimulating and managing collaborative relationships. Yet it is clear from observing organizations such as those using the Scanlon Plan not only that it is possible to establish collaborative relationships, even between labor and management, but also that where this has been done, organizational and group effectiveness have been as high as or higher than under competitive conditions.

THE PROBLEM OF INTEGRATION IN PERSPECTIVE

I have discussed two basic issues in this chapter, both dealing with psychological groups: (1) the development of groups within organizations which can fulfill both the needs of the organization and the psychological needs of its members; and (2) the problems of intergroup competition and conflict. To achieve maximum integration, the organization should be able to create conditions which will facilitate a balance between organizational goals and member needs and which will minimize disintegrative competition between the subunits of the total organization.

Groups are highly complex sets of relationships. There are no easy generalizations about the conditions under which they will be effective, but with suitable training, many kinds of groups can become more effective than they have been. Consequently, group-dynamics training by laboratory methods may be a more promising approach to effectiveness than attempting *a priori* to determine the right membership, type of leadership, and organization. All the factors must be taken into account, with training perhaps weighted more heavily than it has been, though the training itself must be carefully undertaken.

The creation of psychologically meaningful and effective groups does not solve all of the organization's problems if such groups compete and conflict with each other. We examined some of the consequences of competition under win-lose conditions and outlined two basic approaches for dealing with the problem: (1) reducing conflict by increasing communication and locating superordinate goals, and (2) preventing conflict by establishing from the outset organizational conditions which stimulate collaboration rather than competition.

It is important to recognize that the preventive strategy does not imply absence of disagreement and artificial "sweetness and light" within or between groups. Conflict and disagreement at the level of the group or organizational *task* is not only desirable but essential for the achievement of the best solutions to problems. What is harmful is *interpersonal* or *intergroup* conflict in which the task is not as important as gaining advantage over the other person or group. The negative consequences we described, such as mutual negative stereotyping, fall into this latter category and undermine rather than aid over-all task performance. And it is these kinds of conflicts which can be reduced by establishing collaborative relationships. Interestingly enough, observations of cases would suggest that task-relevant conflict which improves over-all effectiveness is greater under collaborative conditions because groups and members trust each other enough to be frank and open in sharing information and opinions. In the competitive situation, each group is committed to hiding its special resources from the other groups, thus preventing effective integration of all resources in the organization.

The Organization
as a Complex System

In Chapter 2, I described the traditional approach to organization and gave as a working definition that an organization is the rational coordination of the activities of a number of people for the achievement of some common explicit purpose through division of labor and a hierarchy of authority. In Chapters 3, 4, and 5, I attempted to show that the internal dynamics of organizations generate forces which are neither predicted by nor very easily integratable into such a definition. The complex interactions between how an individual is inducted into the organization, trained, assigned, and managed; the interaction between the

88

6

formal organization and the various informal groups which arise inevitably within it; the disintegrative forces which formal organizational mechanisms stimulate among subgroups; and the inconsistencies which arise out of assumptions about man which fit formal organizational logic but not the realities of how he functions—all of these points argue for a redefinition of organizations along more dynamic lines. As I have stressed throughout, the complexity and high degree of interaction of the parts of an organization, whether these parts be functions, groups, or individuals, indicate a redefintion in terms of complex systems criteria.

Perhaps the most important argument for a systems conception of organization is that the environment within which organizations exist is becoming increasingly unstable. With the rapid growth of technology, the expansion of economic markets, and rapid social and political change, come constant pressures for organizations to change, adapt, and grow to meet the challenges of the environment. And, as one examines this process, one is struck that it is the total organization, not merely some key individuals, who must be studied if this process is to be properly understood.

The relationships between organizations and their environments are complex and as yet not well conceptualized. First of all, it is difficult to define the appropriate boundaries of any given organization under analysis and to determine what size its environment is. Where does a business concern—with its research departments, suppliers, transportation facilities, sales offices, and public relations offices—leave off and the community begin? Is the relevant environment society as a whole, the economic and political system, other companies in the same market, the immediate community, the union, or all of these?

Secondly, organizations generally have several basic purposes or fulfill multiple functions, some primary, some secondary. The business concern whose ultimate survival depends on making a useful product for a profit may have as a secondary function the provision of secure, adequately paid, meaningful jobs for its community. The cultural and social norms which dictate this secondary function are just as much a part of the relevant environment as are the economic forces which demand a good product at minimum cost. Yet these sets of forces may impose conflicting demands on the organization. When the organization has several primary functions, as does, say, a university-connected hospital, the differential pressures from different parts of the environment may be even more acute and difficult to conceptualize.

Thirdly, the organization carries within itself representatives of the external environment. Employees are not only members of the organization which employs them, but they are also members of society, other organizations, unions, consumer groups, and so on. From these various other roles they bring with them demands, expectations, and cultural norms. How should an organization theorist describe a system which carries representatives of its external environment within itself?

My point in mentioning these difficulties is to warn you that theory in this area is imperfect and incomplete. Systems conceptions take us much farther in clarifying organizations than did the simple mechanical models of early organization theory, but they still leave much to be desired. Having said this, let us examine some proposed conceptual scheme to illustrate the type of theory toward which, I believe, we must move.

The Tavistock Model [1]

Some of the most vigorous proponents of the systems approach to organizational phenomena have been the group of social scientists associated with the Tavistock Institute in London. Out of their studies of changing technology in the coal mining industry and the redesign of work in Indian textile mills, they developed, first, the important concept of the socio-technical system and then the more general open-system definition of organizations.

The idea of a socio-technical system as put forth by Trist implies that any productive organization or part thereof is a combination of technology (task requirements, physical layout, equipment available) and a social system (a system of relationships among those who must perform the job). The technology and the social system are in mutual interaction with each other and each determines the other. In keeping with this concept, it would make just as little sense to say that the nature of the work will *determine* the nature of the organization which develops among workers as it would to say that the socio-psychological characteristics of the workers will *determine* the manner in which a given job will be performed. As the Hawthorne studies and Trist's coal-mining studies have shown (see Chapter 3), each determines the other to some degree.

The open-system model of organizations as discussed by Rice argues that any given organization "imports" various things from its environment, utilizes these imports in some kind of "conversion" process, and then "exports" products, services, and "waste materials" which result from the conversion process. One important import is the information obtained from the environment pertaining to the primary task—that is, what the organization *must* do in order to survive. Other imports are the raw materials, money, equipment, and people involved in the conversion to something which is exportable and meets some environmental demands.

If we now combine these two ideas, we can see the importance of multiple channels of interaction between the environment and the organization. Not only must the organization deal with the demands and constraints imposed by the environment on raw materials, money, and consumer preferences, but it must also deal with the expectations, values, and norms of the people who must operate the work organization. The capacities, preferences, and expectations of the employee are, from this point of view, not merely something he brings with him; they are also something which is influenced by the

---

[1] I have labelled this section the Tavistock model because of the many people involved in formulating this model. Most of the material discussed is drawn from two primary sources: (1) E.L. Trist *et al. Organizational choice.* London: Tavistock Publications, 1963. (2) A.K. Rice. *The enterprise and its environment.* London: Tavistock Publications, 1963.

nature of the job and the organizational structure during his working career. Consequently, one cannot solve the problem merely by better selection or training techniques. Rather, the initial design of the organization must take into account both the nature of the job (the technical system) and the nature of the people (the social system).

For example, in the coal mining studies previously cited, if it is true that mining induces anxiety and that anxiety can best be managed in small cohesive work groups, then a technology which prevents such work group formation is likely to be ineffective. On the other hand, if one starts with the concept of open socio-technical systems, one would ask, "What *combination* of technology, initial worker characteristics, and organizational structures would most likely result in an effective work organization?"

An answer to this question might require the reassessment of the relative importance of different environmental inputs relative to the basic task. Economic demands and technological developments might both argue for a work method and structure which undermines the social system. The organization planner might then have to reassess whether the gains of an effective social organization in terms of long-run economic gains outweigh the gains of short-run maximum efficiency. In order to make this reassessment, he would have to consider a variety of other environmental characteristics—for example, changing aspects of the labor force, particularly on key variables like anxiety proneness; technology in related fields, such as methods of improving mine safety; trends in labor-management relations and union policies; and so on.

The Homans Model [2]

One especially useful model of social systems, whether at the level of the small group or large organization, has been proposed by the sociologist George Homans. This model, as we will see, is not fundamentally at odds with the Tavistock model, but is somewhat more differentiated and complex. Any social system exists within a three-part environment: a *physical* environment (the terrain, climate, layout, and so on), a *cultural* environment (the norms, values, and goals of society), and a *technological* environment (the state of knowledge and instrumentation available to the system for the performance of its task). The environment imposes or specifies certain activities and interactions for the people involved in the system. These activities and interactions in turn arouse certain feelings and sentiments among the people toward each other and the environment. The combination of activities, interactions, and sentiments which are primarily determined by the environment are called the *external system*.

Homans postulates that activities, interactions, and sentiments are mutually dependent on one another. Thus, any change in any of the three variables will produce some change in the other two; in some cases, the direction of the change can be specified. Of particular interest, here, is the relationship postulated between interaction and sentiments, which is that *the higher the rate of interaction of two or more people, the more positive will be their sentiments toward each other*. Or vice versa: the more positive the sentiment, the higher the rate of interaction. The seemingly obvious exception of two people

[2] G.C. Homans. *The human group.* New York: Harcourt, Brace & World, 1950.

who come to hate each other as a result of interacting is explained if we realize that over the long run these people will reduce their interaction as much as possible. If they are forced into continued interaction, they often find good sides to each other so that positive sentiment in the end grows with increased interaction.

Whether propositions such as the one cited are true or false is, for the moment, not as important as the dynamic conceptualization which Homans provides, because from it can be derived several other important concepts. Homans notes that with increasing interaction come not only new sentiments which were not necessarily specified by the external environment, but also new norms and shared frames of reference which generate new activities, also not specified by the external environment. In the Hawthorne studies, it was found that the workers developed games, interaction patterns, and sentiments which were not suggested and not even sanctioned by the environment. Homans has called this new pattern which arises out of the external system, the *internal system*. The internal system corresponds to what most theorists have labelled the informal organization.

Homans further postulates that the internal and external systems are mutually dependent. This means that any change in either system will produce some change in the other. A change in the work technology will produce a change in patterns of interaction, which in turn will change (or sometimes temporarily destroy) the internal system. (The longwall coal mining method destroyed some of the primary work groups.) On the other hand, if the internal system develops certain norms about how life should be organized, it will often change the way the work is actually performed, how much of it will be done, and what quality will result. (The members of the bank-wiring room developed patterns of job trading, a concept of a fair day's output, and their own leadership.)

Finally, the two systems and the environment are mutually dependent. Just as changes in the environment will produce changes in the formal and informal work organization, so the norms and activities developed in the internal system will eventually alter the physical, technical, and cultural environment. For example, out of workers' informal problem-solving may come ideas for technological innovations (change in technical environment), redesigned work layouts (change in physical environment), and new norms about the nature of the psychological contract between workers and management (change in cultural environment).

The most important aspect of this conceptual scheme is its explicit recognition of the various mutual dependencies. Empirical research studies have shown again and again how events in one part of the organization turn out to be linked to events in other parts or in the environment. Similarly, consultants have found how changes in one part of an organization produce unanticipated and often undesired changes in other parts. Conceptualizations such as those of Homans, Trist, and Rice make it possible to analyze and anticipate such events.

Likert's model of organizations adds two important ideas to the models already presented. First, organizations can be usefully conceptualized as systems of interlocking groups; and second, the interlocking groups are connected by individuals who occupy key positions of dual membership, serving as linking pins between groups.

This conception does not conflict with either of the above, but it draws our attention to two important points. First, the relevant environment for any given group or system is likely to be, not something impersonal, but rather a set of other systems or groups. This set is composed of three parts: (1) larger-scale systems, such as the whole complex of organizations performing a similar job or society as a whole; (2) systems on the same level, such as other organizations like itself, consumer and supplier organizations, community groups, and so on; and (3) subsystems within the given system, such as the formal and informal work groups.

Second, the organization is linked to its environment through key people who occupy positions in both the organization and some environmental system, and the parts of the environment may well be linked to each other through similar key people. To the extent that this model is correct, it suggests not only a relevant point of entry in analyzing system-environment relations (the location of linking pins), but also implies that the parts of the environment are not independent of each other. Consequently, if an organization is to understand and deal with its environment, it must seek out and understand these interdependencies.

Katz and Lazarsfeld's analysis of the "two-step" flow of communication provides a good example of the point I am trying to make here.[4] These investigators discovered that influence on consumer beliefs and preferences does not result from direct exposure of the individual to relevant information and advertising, but rather from exposure to "opinion leaders" in the community. Thus, if an opinion leader in the realm of fashions or political beliefs changed his outlook, a great many individual consumers would follow suit. The effect of advertising on the opinion leader is therefore the critical variable.

If this phenomenon is indeed general, it argues that a business must sell to the opinion leaders in its environment, not to its individual consumers. These leaders then can act as linking pins between the organization and its clients or consumers. Similarly, if several consumer groups are involved and their opinion leaders influence each other, it is important for the selling organization to know that the two groups are not independent portions of the environment. It it influences one, it may influence the other as well.

---

[3] Likert's theory is most clearly presented in R. Likert. *New patterns of management.* New York: McGraw-Hill, 1961. The concept as expounded there deals primarily with the internal relationships among parts of the organization. However, the conceptualization is also useful in thinking about organization-environment relationships, hence I am extending it to this other focus.

[4] E. Katz and P.F. Lazarsfeld. *Personal influence.* Glencoe, Ill.: The Free Press, 1955.

The Kahn Overlapping-Role-Set Model [5]

Robert Kahn and his colleagues have pointed out that while the overlapping-group model is closer to organizational reality, it still misses the important point that psychological groups and formal groups may be different. In Likert's model, no clear provision is made for distinguishing between types of groups, and thereby accurately identifying the linking pins. Kahn has proposed that instead of groups, one should consider what sociologists have termed "role sets." If one considers the formal positions in an organization as "offices," and the behavior expected of any person occupying an office as his "role," one can then ask, "What other offices are linked to the particular one under consideration in the operating organization?" Or, to put it in terms of the role concept, one can ask, "Given a focal person fulfilling an organizational role, with whom else is he connected or associated in performing his role?" The set of people—superiors, subordinates, peers, and outsiders—with whom he has role-related relationships then constitutes his "role set." The organization as a whole can then be thought of as a set of overlapping and interlocking role sets, some of which transcend the boundaries of the organization.

The behavior of members of an organization can then be studied in terms of the concept of either role *conflict*—where different members of the role set expect different things of the focal person—or role *ambiguity*—where members of the role set fail to communicate to the focal person information he feels he needs to have in order to perform his role, either because they do not have the information or because they withhold it. The kinds of expectations which members of the role set hold, the manner in which they attempt to influence the focal person, his perceptions of their expectations and influence attempts, his feelings and reactions to these, and his attempts to cope with the feelings and tensions which may be generated—these can then be related to organizational factors (rank, type of job, reward system, and so on), to personality factors in the focal person or the role senders, and to interpersonal factors which characterize the nature of the relationship between role senders and the focal person (degree of trust, relative power, dependence, and so forth).

For example, in their study, Kahn and his colleagues show that role conflict will be greater if the role set includes some members who are inside and some who are outside the organizational boundaries; role conflict and ambiguity also tend to be greater the higher the rank of the focal person in the organization structure; coping responses of the person who experiences tension as a result of role conflict or ambiguity often reduce tension but at the expense of organizational effectiveness. For example, the person who perceives conflict may deal with it by ignoring or denying some of the legitimate expectations which some members of his role set have communicated, resulting in a portion of the job remaining undone. People do not attempt to resolve the conflict by bringing together the role senders whose demands are conflicting, thus making it impossible to achieve an integrative solution.

[5] R.L. Kahn, D.M. Wolfe, R.P. Quinn, J.D. Snoek, and R.A. Rosenthal. *Organizational stress: studies in role conflict and ambiguity.* New York: Wiley, 1964.

The point which Kahn's study underlines is again the great degree of interdependence of organizational variables like rank, location of position in the structure, role expectations, perceptions of such expectations, coping patterns in response to perceived conflict, and effectiveness of role performance. Kahn's focus on the concept of role also highlights the possibility that more abstract concepts of organization (for instance, overlapping role-sets) are amenable to empirical research.

To summarize, I have attempted to show in the above several examples of theorizing about organizations the trend toward systems-level concepts which take into account the interactions and mutual dependencies of internal organizational and environmental variables. If one attempts to build a definition of organization in terms of such concepts, one must go beyond the traditional one with which we started.

TOWARD A REDEFINITION OF ORGANIZATION

I will not attempt to give a tight definition of organization in systems terms because this cannot as yet be done. Instead, I will attempt to highlight where a new definition has to enlarge upon or change the traditional one.

First, the organization must be conceived of as an open system, which means that it is in constant interaction with its environment, taking in raw materials, people, energy, and information, and transforming or converting these into products and services which are exported into the environment.

Second, the organization must be conceived of as a system with multiple purposes or functions which involve multiple interactions between the organization and its environment. Many of the activities of subsystems within the organization cannot be understood without considering these multiple interactions and functions.

Third, the organization consists of many subsystems which are in dynamic interaction with one another. Instead of analyzing organizational phenomena in terms of individual behavior, it is becoming increasingly important to analyze the behavior of such subsystems, whether they be conceived in terms of groups, roles, or some other concept.

Fourth, because the subsystems are mutually dependent, changes in one subsystem are likely to affect the behavior of other subsystems.

Fifth, the organization exists in a dynamic environment which consists of other systems, some larger, some smaller than the organization. The environment places demands upon and constrains the organization in various ways. The total functioning of the organization cannot be understood, therefore, without explicit consideration of these environmental demands and constraints.

Finally, the multiple links between the organization and its environment make it difficult to specify clearly the boundaries of any given organization. Ultimately, a concept of organization is perhaps better given in terms of the stable *processes* of import, conversion, and export, rather than characteristics such as size, shape, function, or structure.

Given a systems concept of organization, how does one assess how well or poorly the system is functioning? This will be the topic of our next and final chapter.

Organizational
Effectiveness

Throughout the previous chapters, we have referred to organizational effectiveness but have not faced up explicitly to the question of just how to define what is effective and what is not. Early theories of organization were content to talk of "profit maximization," "providing an efficient service," "high productivity," and "good employee morale," as sufficient criteria of effectiveness. What has undermined these as viable criteria has been (1) the discovery that seemingly rational organizations behave ineffectively if the sole criterion is profit or providing a good service, and (2) the discovery that organizations fulfill multiple functions and

7

have multiple goals, some of which may be in conflict with each other. For example, if we think of organizations like universities, teaching hospitals, or prisons, we can immediately name several functions or goals, all of which are primary and essential. The university must teach and, at the same time, must create valid knowledge through research; the teaching hospital must take care of and cure patients, and must provide learning opportunities for interns and residents; the prison must keep criminals out of circulation, and must provide opportunities for rehabilitation. Is the effectiveness of the organization to be judged by its performance on one function, on both separately, or on some integration of the several functions?

One attempted resolution to these dilemmas has been to define effectiveness in terms of systems-level criteria. Acknowledging that every system has multiple functions and that it exists within an environment which provides unpredictable inputs, a system's effectiveness can be defined as its capacity to survive, adapt, maintain itself, and grow, regardless of the particular functions it fulfills. A number of students of organization such as Argyris, Trist, Rice, and Bennis have argued explicitly for this type of conception. Perhaps the clearest statement of effectiveness criteria in these terms has been given by Bennis.[1] He introduces these ideas in reference to the traditional approaches of measuring output and satisfaction at a given point in time:

> If we view organizations as adaptive, problem-solving, organic structures, then inferences about effectiveness have to be made, not from static measures of output, though these may be helpful, but on the basis of the processes through which the organization approaches problems. In other words, no single measurement of organizational efficiency or satisfaction—no single time slice of organizational performance—can provide valid indicators of organizational health.

Instead, Bennis proposes the following three criteria of health, criteria which, interestingly, closely mirror recent formulations about mental health proposed by Jahoda: [2]

1. *Adaptability*—the ability to solve problems and to react with flexibility to changing environmental demands.

2. *A sense of identity*—knowledge and insight on the part of the organization of what it is, what its goals are, and what it is to do. Pertinent questions are: to what extent are goals understood and shared widely by members of the organization, and to what extent is self-perception on the part of organization members in line with perceptions of the organization by others?

3. *Capacity to test reality*—the ability to search out, accurately perceive, and correctly interpret the real properties of the environment, particularly those which have relevance for the functioning of the organization.

A fourth criterion which is often mentioned, one which in effect underlies the others, is a state of "integration" among the subparts of the total organization, such that the parts are not working at cross-purposes. For Argyris, for

[1] W.G. Bennis. Toward a "truly" scientific management: the concept of organizational health. *General Systems Yearbook,* 1962, 7, 269–82. Quotation from p. 273.

[2] Marie Jahoda. *Current concepts of positive mental health.* New York: Basic Books, 1958.

example, this criterion is central, and he devotes most of his research and theorizing to finding those conditions which will permit an integration of individual needs and organizational goals.[3] What he regards as unhealthy or ineffective are restrictions on output, destructive competition, and apathy among employees in order to fulfill personal needs at the expense of organizational goals.

McGregor has argued in a similar vein for the integration of personal and organizational goals.[4] According to his theory, if management develops practices built on a more valid set of assumptions about man (those mentioned in Chapter 4 under the concept of complex man), it will produce this integration and hence greater effectiveness. Finally, Blake and Mouton [5] argue for the integration of concern for production and concern for people. Organizational effectiveness, according to Blake and Mouton, is achieved when management succeeds in being both production- and people-centered. To support this theory, they have developed training programs which explicitly attempt to develop this managerial style. In summary, a systems-level criterion of organizational effectiveness must be a *multiple* criterion involving adaptability, sense of identity, capacity to test reality, and internal integration.

To the extent that effectiveness is a *multiple* criterion, we need to be careful to avoid the trap of concluding that it depends on merely one thing. Thus, it would be a mistake to assume that if one selected the right people and trained them to do the job, effectiveness would be insured. It would be equally erroneous to assume that the establishment of a mutually satisfactory psychological contract with employees, or the reduction of intergroup competition, or leadership training, any of these alone, would guarantee effectiveness. Rather, the systems conception leads us to a different way of thinking about the problem: Viewed as a total system, how does an organization cope with its environment? How does it obtain information and process it validly? What mechanisms exist for translating information, particularly about alterations in the environment, into changed operations? Are the internal operations flexible enough to cope with changes?

MAINTAINING EFFECTIVENESS
THROUGH AN ADAPTIVE-COPING CYCLE

The sequence of activities or processes which begin with some change in the internal or external environment and end with a more adaptive dynamic equilibrium for dealing with the change is the organization's *adaptive-coping cycle*. If we identify the various stages or processes of this cycle, we will also be able to identify the points where organizations typically may fail to cope adequately and where, therefore, consultants and researchers have been able in a variety of ways to help increase organizational effectiveness.

[3] C. Argyris. *Integrating the individual and the organization.* New York: Wiley, 1964.
[4] D. McGregor. *The human side of enterprise.* New York: McGraw-Hill, 1960.
[5] R.R. Blake and Jane S. Mouton. *The managerial grid.* Houston, Tex.: Gulf Publishing Co., 1964.

The stages of the adap-
tive-coping cycle are six-fold, as follows:

1. Sensing a change in the internal or external environment.
2. Importing the relevant information about the change into those parts of the organization which can act upon it.
3. Changing production or conversion processes inside the organization according to the information obtained.
4. Stabilizing internal changes while reducing or managing undesired by-products (undesired changes in related systems which have resulted from the desired changes).
5. Exporting new products, services, and so on, which are more in line with the originally perceived changes in the environment.
6. Obtaining feedback on the success of the change through further sensing of the state of the external environment and the degree of integration of the internal environment.

Let us illustrate this process with two simple examples. Suppose a manufacturing concern producing electronic equipment learns that the space program is going to increase the demand for this equipment a great deal (stage 1). The information about this change in demand must be imported into the organization in the sense of being taken seriously by those members who are in a position to do something about it. It is not sufficient for the market research department to have the information if it cannot convince the general management (stage 2). If management becomes convinced, it must change its production processes to enable the company to produce more of the equipment (stage 3). These changes must be accomplished without producing other undesirable internal changes (for example, a strike in response to unreasonable demands for increased production) and they must be stabilized (stage 4). The increased production must be marketed and sold (stage 5). And, finally, sales figures and future-demand figures must then be analyzed to determine whether the organizational change has been "successful" in terms of increased marketability, and the internal environment must be assessed to determine whether unanticipated costs in the form of lowered morale or intergroup competition have been minimized (stage 6).

For a different example, let us take a college fraternity as the organization. The fraternity leadership might sense in the college administration a shift in policy toward shutting down fraternities unless scholastic standards increase (stage 1). Stage 2 would then be to get the membership to recognize the real danger to the survival of the fraternity. Stage 3 might be a program of changing norms by reducing emphasis on social activities and increasing emphasis on scholastic activities, without (stage 4) producing undesired changes such as total loss of prestige among other fraternities. In connection with these stages the fraternity leaders might also recognize the necessity of convincing *other* fraternities on the campus to develop similar programs in their own houses, because of the likelihood that university policy would respond only to changes in the whole fraternity system. Stage 5 would be the actual improvement in grades, test performance, and classroom behavior, while stage 6 would be a matter of checking with the administration about whether the fraternity's standing was improving, whether policy would again change, and what fraternity member attitudes now were.

Both examples cited start with some changes in the external environment. The coping cycle is no different, however, if the first step is the recognition that something is not right in the *internal* environment. Thus, an organization may sense that employee morale is too low, or that several departments are destructively competing with one another, or that a technologically sound process is not being used correctly in production, or that management attitudes and practices are failing to elicit adequate motivation and loyalty among the employees. Once the information of some change or problem is sensed by some part of the organization, it must then be imported and lead to changes in the manner described if organizational effectiveness is to be increased.

Problems and Pitfalls
in the Adaptive-Coping Cycle

One advantage of considering the adaptive-coping cycle as a series of stages lies in helping to identify areas of difficulty in maintaining and improving effectiveness in response to a changing environment. Certain problems and pitfalls characteristically are associated with each stage.

1. *Failure to sense changes in the environment or incorrectly sensing what is happening.* There are innumerable cases of organizations which have failed to survive because they did not sense either a decline in the demand for their product or an important internal problem. Many businesses can adjust to new conditions provided the organization can sense when the time is ripe to develop new products, or services, or procedures. If the organization has multiple functions, as does a university, it becomes especially important to accurately sense changing attitudes about education, the role of the university in the community, the feelings of alumni about contributions, the reputation it enjoys within the academic community, the morale of its faculty, and so on. Consulting and applied research specialities like market research, consumer psychology, and public opinion polling have developed partly in response to organizational needs for more accurate sensing of internal and external environmental changes.

2. *Failure to get the relevant information to those parts of the organization which can act upon it or use it.* One of the commonest problems of present-day large-scale organizations is that staff units within them obtain information which they are unable to impart to line management. For example, many personnel departments have become convinced that the management process would be more effective if line management would adopt assumptions about the nature of man consistent with the findings reported in Chapter 4. One could say that the personnel departments have correctly sensed a change in the state of research knowledge concerning the management process. But unless this knowledge can be imparted in a meaningful way to line managers,

one cannot say that the information has really been imported into the system. This example illustrates another difficulty. To change assumptions about the nature of man involves a change of attitudes, self-images, and working procedures. Such a change will typically be strongly resisted because of its threatening nature. Any change implies that the former way of functioning has been erroneous. To get the information imported, therefore, might involve a major and lengthy program of influencing attitudes, self-images, and working procedures.

Often a research department or other unit of an organization comes upon information which argues for changes in technology, production methods, and the like, yet is unable to convince key management to consider the information seriously. Difficulties in introducing automatic data-processing equipment into various organizational departments often stem from a refusal of management to pay attention to information on how the equipment would really work because the implied change is too threatening to established ways of working, attitudes, and basic assumptions.

These difficulties of importing information into the relevant system have led to the use of external consultants or researchers as information transmitters. A staff group which already correctly senses a problem may find itself hiring a consultant to re-identify the problem and import it to other parts of the system. The consultant uses his prestige to help import the information into those parts of the system that have the power to do something about it.

3. *Failure to influence the conversion or production system to make the necessary changes.* Effecting internal changes in an organization requires more than the recognition that such changes are necessary. Organization planners or top managers often naively assume that simply announcing the need for a change and giving orders that the change should be made will produce the desired outcome. In practice, however, resistance to change is one of the most ubiquitous organizational phenomena. Whether it be an increase in production which is desired, or adaptation to a new technology, or a new method of doing the work, it is generally found that those workers and managers who are directly affected will resist the change or sabotage it if it is forced upon them. The Trist coal mining studies cited in Chapter 3 offer one good example of this process.

Probably the major reason for resistance to change is that the conversion or production parts of any organization are themselves systems—they generate ways of working, stable interpersonal relationships, common norms and values, and techniques of coping and surviving in their own environment. In other words, the subsystems of an organization operate by the same coping principles as the whole organization. In order to change, therefore, the subsystem must sense a change in management policy, be able to import this information into itself, manage its own change, stabilize it, export better results in terms of the desires of management, and obtain feedback on how it is doing. The line manager desiring the change can, from this point of view, accomplish more by viewing his own role as that of helping the system to change or cope, rather than giving orders or issuing directives. There is some evidence that one of the best ways of giving this help is to involve the system concerned in the decision-making about *how* to produce the necessary changes. The more the system which must change participates in decisions about how to manage the change, the less likely it is to resist the change and the more stable the change is likely to be.[6]

4. *Failure to consider the impact of changes on other systems and failure to achieve stable change.* In Chapter 3, we cited some classic cases where attitudes changed during a program of training in human relations but reverted completely following a return to the job. Cases can also be cited where changes in administrative procedure in one department were so threatening to another department that they had to be abandoned to preserve the over-all morale of the organization.[7] Because the various parts of an organization tend to be linked, a proposed change in one part must be carefully assessed in terms of its likely impact on other parts. Wherever possible, the linkage between systems should be used to positive advantage, in the sense that certain desired changes, if started in one part of the system, will tend to spread by themselves to other parts of the system.

A good example of this process would be in the changing of assumptions about and attitudes toward people. If the top management of the organization can be helped to alter attitudes, then because of their strategic linkage to all parts of the organization, their resultant behavior change would automatically act as a force on all of their subordinates toward similar changes. The same change in attitudes in the middle or near the bottom of the hierarchy may fail to spread or even to maintain itself because of inadequate upward and lateral linkages to other systems.

5. *Failure to export the new product, service, or information.* Once changes have been made within the organization, there remains the problem of exporting the new results. In the case of business concerns, this is a problem of sales and marketing. In the case of other organizations, such as the fraternity cited above, it may be a problem of communicating as rapidly as possible to the relevant environmental systems the changes which have occurred. It does little good for the fraternity to change its norms of scholastic achievement if the time before grades improve is so long that the administration has already decided to close the fraternities.

If the organization wants to export information, the problem is one of advertising. But because advertising involves gaining a competitive advantage over another organization, forces toward distorting information are generated. Here, as in the above cases, one role the consultant has played has been to export *reliable* information about changes in the system. Thus, a neutral faculty member may be appointed jointly by the administration and the fraternity to evaluate changes in members' attitudes. Similarly, we send "political observers" to countries requesting foreign aid to evaluate the validity of their claims that they are changing toward democratic forms of govern-

[6] K. Lewin. Group decision and social change. In Eleanor Maccoby, T. Newcomb, and E. Hartley (eds.). *Readings in social psychology*. New York: Holt, Rinehart, and Winston, 1958. Also, L. Coch and J.R.P. French. Overcoming resistance to change. *Hum. Relat.*, 1948, 1, 512–532.

[7] A. Bavelas and G. Strauss. Group dynamics and intergroup relations. In W. Bennis, K. Benne, and R. Chin (eds.). *The planning of change*. New York: Holt, Rinehart, and Winston, 1962.

ment; government agencies send representatives to industrial firms that claim to have developed the capacity to provide a weapons system or some other product efficiently and cheaply. In all these cases, what is involved is accurate export of information about changes in the system which may not be immediately visible in such indexes as higher production rates or new products and services.

6. *Failure to obtain feedback on the success of the change.* The problems here are essentially the same as the problems of sensing changes in the environment in the first place. We need only add that many organizations have explicitly created systems to assess the impact of changes and thus to provide to themselves the necessary feedback information. In the case of internal changes, there may be a research group in the employee relations department whose prime job is to survey employees periodically to determine how they are reacting to changes in management policy; political organizations will run polls immediately after a change in political platform to determine the public's reaction; production control units will assess whether a new process is producing the desired increase in efficiency; and so on.

In summary, for each stage in the adaptive-coping cycle, one can identify characteristic pitfalls and problems. The important point is that the maintenance and increase of organizational effectiveness depend on successful coping, which means that *all* of the stages must be successfully negotiated somehow. It does little good to have the best market research department in the world if the organization is unable to influence its own production systems; nor does it help to have a highly flexible production or conversion operation which cannot sense or digest information about environmental changes.

ORGANIZATIONAL CONDITIONS FOR EFFECTIVE COPING

We began this chapter with some general criteria of organizational effectiveness or health. We then specified the coping processes which appear to be necessary in a rapidly changing environment for such effectiveness or health to be maintained or increased. In this final section, I would like to outline what internal organizational conditions appear to be necessary for effective coping to occur. To some extent the argument becomes circular here, in that some health must be present for health to maintain itself or increase. The organizational conditions I will identify will, therefore, resemble somewhat the ultimate criteria of health cited by Bennis.

1. Successful coping requires the ability to take in and communicate information reliably and validly.
2. Successful coping requires internal flexibility and creativity to make the changes which are demanded by the information obtained.
3. Successful coping requires integration and commitment to the goals of the organization, from which comes the willingness to change.
4. Successful coping requires an internal climate of support and freedom

from threat, since being threatened undermines good communication, reduces flexibility, and stimulates self-protection rather than concern for the total system.

These four conditions are not easy to achieve in a complex system such as a large organization, but some guidelines for their achievement can be outlined. I would like to present these guidelines in terms of the basic variables provided in the previous chapters.

1. If we look first at the *recruitment, selection, induction, and training of human resources,* we can restate the concern mentioned at the end of Chapter 3. Are many of the methods currently being used for the selection, testing, and training of employees likely to produce an image in the minds of employees that the organization is relatively indifferent to their personal needs and capacities? And is it possible, therefore, that employees learn early in their career to withhold involvement, to make their performance routine, and to respond to demands for changes by feeling threatened and anxious rather than helpful and committed?

If the organization is genuinely concerned about building long-range effectiveness, must it not develop a system for hiring employees which makes them feel wanted, secure, meaningfully engaged in their job, and positively committed to organizational goals, and must it not develop training and management-development programs which stimulate genuine psychological growth in order to insure the flexibility and creativity that may be required at some future time? It would appear that one of the best guarantees of ability to cope with an unpredictable environment would be to develop everyone to a maximum degree, even at the expense of short-run efficiency.

2. Turning next to the *utilization of employees and the psychological contract,* it would appear evident that if the organization expects its members to be committed, flexible, and in good communication with one another for the sake of over-all organizational effectiveness, it is in effect asking them to be *morally* involved in the enterprise, to be committed to organizational goals and to value these. And if it expects them to be involved to this degree, the organization must for its part provide rewards and conditions consistent with such involvement. It cannot merely pay more money to obtain commitment, creativity, and flexibility; there must be the possibility of obtaining non-economic rewards such as autonomy, genuine responsibility, opportunities for challenge and for psychological growth.

Probably the most important thing the organization can do in this regard is to develop assumptions about people which fit reality. This, in turn, implies some willingness to find out what each man is like and what he truly wants. By making broad generalizations about people, the organization not only runs the risk of being wrong about the empirical realities, but, perhaps worse, it insults its employees by assuming they are all basically alike. If managerial assumptions begin to be exposed and tested, not only will this change provide a basis for learning what the facts are, but also the willingness to test assumptions will communicate a degree of concern for people which will reduce their feeling of being threatened or demeaned. As assumptions become increasingly realistic, management practices will begin to build the kind of climate which is needed for reliable and valid communication, creative effort, flexibility, and commitment.

3. Next, let us look at the *problem of groups and intergroup relations.* There is little question that groups are an integral part of any organization and that the basic choice is not whether to have them but, rather, how to create conditions under which group forces work toward organizational goals rather than counter to them. The first part of an answer is to be found in points 1 and 2 above, for the evidence seems quite clear that if employees feel threatened, demeaned, and unappreciated they will form together into *anti-*management groups. To prevent such groups from forming, therefore, requires management practices which are less threatening to the individual and more likely to enable him to integrate his own needs with organizational goals.

A second part of the answer lies in training for effective group membership and leadership. Though most of us have had much experience in groups, it is unlikely that we have had the opportunity to focus clearly on those factors which make groups more or less effective. If members of the organization come to understand better how groups work, they are less likely to form groups which are bound to fail. If groups are formed which can achieve some degree of psychological success, and if this success is perceived to be in part the result of good management, the group forces are more likely to be turned toward organizational goals. The point is, however, that it takes more than good intentions to make an effective group. It requires knowledge and training of how groups work.

When we turn to problems of intergroup competition, the answer seems clear that competition between the units or groups of a single organization or system must in the long run reduce effectiveness because competition leads to faulty communication, to greater pressures for conformity and hence less flexibility, and to commitment to subgroup rather than organizational goals. The dilemma is that competition also produces very high levels of motivation and productivity. As many case examples have shown, however, when organizational units are stimulated into competition, the short-run gains of increased production are greatly outweighed by the long-run losses of reduced internal communication and flexibility. What organizations must develop is programs which obtain motivation and commitment in an integrative manner, which keep communication channels between subparts open, and which maintain the focus on total, organizational performance rather than individual, subgroup performance.

4. Finally, let us look at a variable which has been implicit throughout, but has not been explicitly treated—the variable of *leadership.* Much has been written on leadership and it is beyond the scope of this discussion to review even cursorily the mass of research findings and theoretical positions which have been published. Two points are worth noting, however.

First, leadership is a *function* in the organization, rather than the trait of an individual. It is *distributed among the members of a group or organization,* and is not automatically vested in the chairman or the person with the formal authority. Good leadership and good membership therefore blend into each other in an effective organization. It is just as much the task of a member to help the group reach its goals as it is the task of the formal leader.

Second, leadership has a unique obligation to manage the relationships between a system and its environment, particularly in reference to the key functions of setting goals for the organization and defining the values or norms in terms of which the organization must basically develop a sense of identity.[8] This function must be fulfilled by those members who are in contact with the organization-environment boundary and who have the power to set policy for the organization. This leadership function, which usually falls to the top executives of organizations, is critical. If the organization does not have clear goals and cannot develop a sense of identity, there is nothing to be committed to and nothing to communicate. At the same time, no organization need have its goals and identity *imposed* by its top executives. There is no reason why the organization cannot develop its goals and identity collaboratively and participatively, engaging every member down to the lowest echelons. What the top executives must do is to insure that goals are set somehow, but they may choose a variety of ways of allowing this to occur.

CONCLUSION

I have tried to argue for an approach to organizational effectiveness which hinges upon good communication, flexibility, creativity, and genuine psychological commitment. These conditions are to be obtained by (1) recruitment, selection, and training practices which stimulate rather than demean people; (2) more realistic psychological relationships based on a more realistic psychological contract; (3) more effective group action; and (4) better leadership in the sense of goal-setting and value-definition. The argument is not based on the assumption that this would be nice for people or make them feel better. Rather, the argument is that systems *work better* if their parts are in good communication with each other, are committed, and are creative and flexible.

[8] P. Selznick. *Leadership in administration.* Evanston, Ill.: Row-Peterson, 1957.

Selected Readings

Allbright, L., J. Glennon, and W. Smith. *The use of psychological tests in industry*. Cleveland: Howard Allen, 1963.

Argyris, C. *Integrating the individual and the organization*. New York: Wiley, 1964.

Blau, P., and W. R. Scott. *Formal organizations*. San Francisco: Chandler, 1962.

Costello, T., and S. Zalkind. *Psychology in administration*. Englewood Cliffs, N. J.: Prentice-Hall, 1963.

Fleishman, E. *Studies in personnel and industrial psychology*. Homewood, Ill.: Dorsey, 1961.

Haire, M. *Psychology in management* (2nd ed.). New York: McGraw-Hill, 1964.

Herzberg, F., B. Mausner, and B. Snyderman. *The motivation to work*. New York: Wiley, 1959.

Kahn, R., D. Wolfe, R. Quinn, J. D. Snoek, and R. Rosenthal. *Organizational stress*. New York: Wiley, 1964.

Leavitt, H. J. *Managerial psychology*. Chicago: University of Chicago Press, 1958.

Leavitt, H. J. (ed.). *The social science of organizations*. Englewood Cliffs, N. J.: Prentice-Hall, 1963.

Levinson, H., C. Price, K. Munden, H. Mandl, and C. Solley. *Men, management, and mental health*. Cambridge, Mass.: Harvard University Press, 1962.

Likert, A. *New patterns of management*. New York: McGraw-Hill, 1961.

March, J. *A handbook of organizations*. New York: Rand-McNally (in press).

March, J., and H. Simon. *Organizations*. New York: Wiley, 1958.

McGregor, D. *The human side of enterprise.* New York: McGraw-Hill, 1960.

Rice, A. K. *The enterprise and its environment.* London: Tavistock, 1963.

Schein, E. H., and W. G. Bennis. *Personal and organizational change through group methods.* New York: Wiley, 1965.

Stagner, R. *The psychology of industrial conflict.* New York: Wiley, 1956.

Tannenbaum, R., I. Weschler, and F. Mawwarik. *Leadership and organization.* New York: McGraw-Hill, 1961.

Trist, E., G. Higgin, H. Murray, and A. Pollock. *Organizational choice.* London: Tavistock, 1963.

Vroom, V. *Work and motivation.* New York: Wiley, 1964.

Warner, W., and N. Martin. *Industrial man.* New York: Harper & Row, 1959.

Whyte, W. *Money and motivation.* New York: Harper & Row, 1955.

Index

A

Absenteeism, 52
Adams, J. S., 65n
Adaptive-coping cycle, for maintaining organizational effectiveness, 98–106:
conditions for effective coping, guidelines, 103–106
problems and pitfalls in, 100–103
stages of the cycle, 99–100
Affiliation needs, 70
Air Force, 21
Alienation of employees, 10, 45–46, 61–63
Allocation of human resources, 9–10, 26–34, 72
Anomie, 31
Antimanagement groups, 28–30, 33, 77, 105
Application blank, 22
Argyris, C., 33, 56, 58, 61n, 97–98
Army, organizational systems, 7–8, 13, 71, 72
Assembly lines, 50, 53, 58, 62, 69
Authority:
bases of, 11–13
charismatic basis for, 12–13
coercive power, 45
hierarchy of, 8, 11, 43
rational-legal basis for, 12, 44, 45, 47
tradition as basis for, 12
Autocratic organizations, 44
Automation, 16
Autonomy, for employees, 59, 62, 104

B

Barnard, C., 8
Base rate, 20
Benevolent autocracies, 44
Bennis, W. G., 61*n*, 97
Blake, R. R., 83, 84, 98
Blauner, R., 62
Bureau of Internal Revenue, 15

C

Calculative-utilitarian contract, 58
Cause-effect relationships, 4
Charisma, as basis for authority, 12–13
Chinese Communists, indoctrination program for prisoners of war, 69
Cliques, 69
Coal mining, Tavistock Institute studies, 30–32, 50, 90, 91, 92, 101
Coercive power, 45
Collaborative relations among groups, 80
Collective bargaining, 47 (*see also* Unions)
College graduates, early job experiences of, 36
Commonweal organizations, 15
Communications, 78, 93, 100–101, 104
Competition among groups within organization, 3, 4, 14–15, 80–85, 99, 105
Complex-man theory, 60–63, 73, 98:
    evidence for, 61–63
    in groups, 73
    implied managerial strategy, 60–61
Consent, of worker to authority, 11–13
Creativity, stimulation of, 16, 106
Criterion, in selection process, *defined,* 19
Cultural environment, 91–92

D

Dalton, M., 69, 71
Defense Department, 15
Design of jobs, 2, 26–34, 72
Dickson, W. J., 27
Differential predictions, 23
Distributive justice in social relationships, 44*n*
Division of labor, 7–8, 13, 43, 85
Dynamic group factors and organizational goals, 71, 74–80:
    oil-refinery labor-management conflict, 74–75, 77

E

Effectiveness of organizations, 15–17, 96–106:
    adaptive-coping cycle, 98–106

Effectiveness of organization (*Cont.*):
    good leadership, 105–106
    systems-level criteria, 97–98
Egalitarian organizations, 44
Employee-centered supervisors, 37, 55, 59
Employees:
    alienation from organization, 10, 45–46, 61–63
    autonomy, 59, 62, 104
    and complex-man theory, 60–63, 73, 98
    dependence of organization on, 41, 50
    image of organization, 3, 32–33, 36, 65, 104
    leader-follower relations, 54–55
    low correlation between short-run and long-run performance, 24
    opportunities for education and self-development, 34
    problems of testing and selection, 23–26
    "rate-busters," 54, 61
    and rational-economic-man theory, 48–50, 51, 56, 60, 72
    recruitment of, 10, 19–23, 104, 106
    "restricters," 54
    and self-actualizing-man theory, 56–60, 62, 72–73
    and social-man theory, 50–56, 57, 60, 72
    superior-subordinate relations, 54–55
    supervisory personnel, training of, 37–40
    training of, 10, 34–42, 75–77, 104, 105, 106
Engineering psychology, 10
Environment, relation of organization to, 2, 15, 71–73, 89–95, 99, 100:
    adjustments to changes in, 2
    external environment, 99, 100
    factors affecting organizational goals, 71–73
    the Homans model, 91–92
    importance of multiple channels of interaction, 90–91
    internal environment, 99, 100
    the Kahn overlapping-role-set model, 94–95
    the Likert overlapping-group model, 93, 94
    the Tavistock model, 90–91
Equalization of power, 64, 77
Ethical limitations of the psychological contract, 25
Etzioni, A., 44–46, 49, 63
External environment, 99, 100
Extrinsic motivation, 57

F

Feedback, importance of, 4, 99, 101, 103
Fleishman, E. A., 38, 54, 55

Foremen, 11, 63 (*see also* Supervisory personnel)
Formal groups, 68
Formal organization, *defined,* 9

G

Gellerman, S. W., 63
Group incentive plans, 51, 54
Groups:
    antimanagement, 28–30, 33, 77, 105
    basic force toward formation of, 67
    cohesiveness, 52–53
    competition among, 3, 14–15, 80–85, 99, 105
    defined, 67–68
    dynamic factors affecting, 71, 74–80
    environmental factors affecting, 71–73
    formal, 68
    functions fulfilled by, 70–71
    group vs. individual performance, 79–80
    history and tradition, 78
    horizontal cliques, 69
    informal, 68–69
    integration of organizational goals and personal needs, 71–80
    intergroup problems in organizations, 80–87
    intergroup relations, 3, 66, 80–87, 105–106
    laboratory methods for training members, 75–77
    leaders' perceptions of members, 78
    the Likert overlapping-group model, 93, 94
    "logical" groups, 72
    membership factors affecting, 71, 73–74
    mixed cliques, 69
    organizational patterns, 78
    problem groups, 73–74
    "random" cliques, 69n
    sensitivity-training groups, 76
    "socio-emotional" leadership, 78–79
    subgroups, 4
    systems of interlocking groups, 93
    "task" leadership, 78–79
    T-groups (training), 76n
    types of, in organizations, 68–69
    vertical cliques, 69
    when to use, 79–80
    win-lose situations in intergroup competition, 82, 85, 86

H

"Hawthorne effect," 27n
Hawthorne studies, 27–30, 37, 38, 50, 58, 69, 92

Herzberg, F., 58–59
Homans, G. C., 91–92
Homans model, 91–92
Horizontal cliques, 69
Human engineering:
    Hawthorne studies, 27–30, 37, 38, 50, 58, 69, 92
    job design, 2, 26–34, 72
    job redesign, 10, 49
    Tavistock Institute coal-mining studies, 30–32, 50, 90, 91, 92, 101
Hygienic factors, 59

I

Image of organization held by employees, 3, 32–33, 36, 65, 104
Incentive systems, 3, 11, 13, 48, 51, 54:
    group incentives 51, 54
Independent work, 55
Individual-organization conflicts, 10
Informal groups, 68–69
Informal organization:
    coal-mining studies, 30–32, 50, 90, 91, 92, 101
    competition between groups, 3, 14–15, 80–85, 99, 105
    defined, 9
    Hawthorne studies, 27–30, 37, 38, 50, 58, 69, 92
    interaction with formal organization, 9
Information-gathering mechanisms, 49
Innovation, 16, 59
Institute of Social Research, University of Michigan, 55
Integration, among parts of organization, 13–15
Interdependent work, 55
Intergroup relations, 66, 105–106:
    competition, 3, 4, 14–15, 80–85, 99, 105
    preventing intergroup conflict, 85–86
    problems in organizations, 80–87
    win-lose situations 82, 85, 86
Interlocking groups, 93
Internal environment, 99, 100
Internal system, 92
International Harvester supervisory training program, 37–38
Interviews, 4, 22, 24
Intrinsic motivation, 57

J

Job allocation, 9–10, 26–34, 72
Job analysis, 2
Job description, 23
Job design, 2, 26–34, 72
Job enlargement, 32

Job redesign, 10, 49
Job simplification, 32

K

Kahn, R. L., 94–95
Kahn overlapping-role-set model, 94–95
Katz, E., 93
Koontz, H., 49
Korean War, combat studies, 53, 69

L

Laboratory training methods:
   of employees for group participation, 75–77, 105
   of reducing intergroup competition, 83–85
Labor-management relations, 81, 91 (*see also* Unions):
   oil-refinery conflict, 74–75, 77
Labor unions (*see* Unions)
Lazarsfeld, P., 93
Leadership:
   laboratory methods of training, 75–77
   opinion leader, 93
   role of, in the organization, 105–106
   "socio-emotional" leadership of groups, 78–79
   "task" leadership of groups, 78–79
Learning, facilitation of, 33–34
Levinson, H., 44
Lieberman, S., 63
Likert, R., 56, 61n, 93, 94
Likert overlapping-group model, 93, 94
Linking pins, 56, 93
"Logical" groups, 72
Longwall coal-mining method, 30–32, 92

M

Managers:
   changing attitudes toward people, 102
   four principle functions, 49
   increasing professionalism of, 5
   linking pins, 56, 93
   managerial climate, 72
   motivational patterns, 62–63
   need for improved selection devices, 23
   need for personal flexibility, 61
   special problems in development of, 37–40
   training of, 40–41
Man-machine systems, 5
Mann, F. C., 61, 62
Marquis, D. G., 79
Maslow, A., 56
Mass production, 53, 58

Mayo, E., 27, 50–51, 52, 56
McGregor, D. M., 33, 48, 56, 61n, 98
Membership factors and organizational goals, 71, 73–74
Michigan studies, 55–56, 59
Mixed cliques, 69
Motivation, 43–65, 72–73, 98:
   changes in, as result of organizational experience, 63
   complex-man theory, 60–63, 73, 98
   extrinsic, 57
   hygienic factors, 59
   incentives and rewards, 3, 10–11, 13, 48, 51, 54
   intrinsic, 57
   management assumption about people, 47–63
   for managers, 62–63
   motivators, 59
   pattern of, 60
   rational-economic-man theory, 48–50, 51, 56, 60, 72
   self-actualizing-man theory, 56–60, 62, 72–73
   social-man theory, 50–56, 57, 60, 72
Motivators, 59
Mouton, J. S., 98
Multiple correlation, 24
Multi-variate analysis, 24
Mutual benefit associations, 15

N

Normative rewards, 45
Norm of reciprocity, 44n
Non-Linear Systems, Inc., 32

O

O'Donnell, C., 49
Oil-refinery labor-management conflict, 74–75, 77
Opinion leader, 93
Organizational psychology, development of the field, 2–5
Organizations:
   adapting to change, 16
   adaptive-coping cycle, 98–106
   adjustments to technological innovations, 2, 4–5
   advertising, 102–103
   allocation of human resources, 9–10, 26–34
   antimanagement groups, 28–30, 33, 77, 105
   authority, bases of, and hierarchy, 8, 11–13, 43, 44, 45, 47
   autocratic, 44
   benevolent autocracies, 44

Organizations (*Cont.*):
    classes of, 15
    communications systems, 78, 93, 100–101, 104
    as a complex system, 88–95
    coordination of effort, 7, 8
    criteria of health, 97–98
    defined, 7–9, 88, 95
    dependence on employees, 41, 50
    division of labor, 7–8, 13, 43, 85
    effectiveness, 15–17, 96–106
    effective use of groups, 73
    egalitarian, 44
    employees (*see* Employees)
    environmental relationships, 2, 15, 71–73, 89–95, 99, 100
    exporting information, 102–103
    feedback, importance of, 4, 99, 101, 103
    groups within (*see* Groups)
    growth of, 15–16
    Homans model, 91–92
    human engineering, 26–34, 37, 38, 50, 58, 69, 90, 92, 101
    individual-organization conflicts, 10
    integration among parts of, 13–15
    intergroup competition, problems of, 3, 4, 14–15, 80–85, 99, 105
    Kahn overlapping-role-set model, 94–95
    leadership (*see* Leadership)
    Likert overlapping-group model, 93, 94
    management assumptions about people, 47–63
    managerial climate, 72
    organizational relationships, types of, 45–47
    paternalistic, 44, 62
    process of management, *defined,* 43
    professionalization of management, 5
    psychological problems in, 6–17
    redefinition of, 95
    subsystems, 4, 36, 40, 93, 95, 101
    system characteristics of, 3
    Tavistock model, 90–91
Output, straight line, 29, 33
Overlapping-group model, 93, 94

P

Paternalistic organizations, 44, 62
Permanent formal groups, 68
Personnel (*see* Employees)
Physical environment, 91–92
Pilot stanine, 21–22
Power equalization, 64, 77
Predictor variables, 20–21
Production-oriented supervisors, 55, 59
Professionalism of management, 5
Profit-sharing plans, 54

Psychological contract, 11–13, 63–65:
    and complex man, 60–63
    ethical limitations, 25
    nature of, 44–47
    and rational-economic man, 49–50
    and self-actualizing man, 57–60
    shift, with organizational complexity, 50
    and social man, 51–56
    violations of, 46–47

Q

Questionnaires, 4

R

"Random" cliques, 69n
"Rate-busters," 54, 61
Rational-economic-man theory, 48–50, 51, 56, 60:
    evidence for, 49–50
    implied managerial strategy, 49
    in informal groups, 72
    and psychological contract, 49
Rational-legal principles, as basis of authority, 12, 44, 45, 47
Reciprocation, 44
Recruitment of personnel, 10, 19–23, 104, 106
Redesign of jobs, 10, 49
Reprimands, 3
Resistance to change, 101
"Restricters," 54
Restriction of output, 28
Reward and punishment systems, 2–3, 45, 46
Rice, A. K., 92, 97
Roethlisberger, F. J., 27, 52
Role-playing, 76
Role sets, 94–95

S

Scanlon, J., 54
Scanlon Plan, 54, 59, 63
Schutz, W., 74n
Seashore, S. F., 52–53
Selection of employees, 2, 10, 19–26, 104, 106:
    improving accuracy of selection, 19–23
    problems of, 23–26
    variables, 22–23
Selection ratio, 20
Self-actualizing-man theory, 56–60, 62, 72–73:
    evidence for, 58–60
    implied managerial strategy, 57–58
    in informal groups, 72–73

Self-actualizing-man theory (*Cont.*):
   and psychological contract, 57–58
Selznick, P., 106
Sensitivity-training groups, 76
Service organizations, 15
Sherif, M., 83
Shortwall method of coal mining, 30
Smith, Adam, 48
Social-man theory, 50–56, 57, 60, 72:
   evidence for, 52–56
   implied managerial strategy, 51–52
   in informal groups, 72
   and psychological contract, 51–52
Social organization, *defined,* 9
"Socio-emotional" leadership of groups,
   78–79
Stanine measure, 21–22
Stewards, union, 63
Straight-line output, 29, 33
Stress interview, 24
Strikes, 44
Subsystems, 4, 36, 40, 93, 95, 101
Suggestion plans, 54
Supervisory personnel (*see also* Man-
   agers):
   conflict resulting from training, 38–40
   employee-centered, 37, 55, 59
   International Harvester supervisory
     training program, 37–38
   production-oriented, 55, 59
   special problems in training of, 37–40
Sykes, A. J. M., 41
Systems point of view in organizational
   psychology:
   forces toward, 4–5
   Homans model, 91–92
   Kahn overlapping-role-set model, 94–
     95
   Likert overlapping-group model, 93,
     94
   organization as complex system, 88–95
   systems-level criteria of organizational
     effectiveness, 97–98
   Tavistock model, 90–91

T

"Task" leadership of groups, 78–79
Tavistock Institute:
   coal-mining studies, 30–32, 50
   Tavistock model, 90–91
Technological environment, 91–92
Technological innovations, organizational
   adjustments to, 2, 4–5
Temporary formal groups, 68
Testing of employees, 19–26:
   problems of, 23–26

T-groups (training), 76n
Theory X, 48
Theory Y, 48, 56n
Time and motion studies, 2, 26
Tradition, as basis of authority, 12
Training of employees, 10, 34–42, 75–77,
   104, 105, 106:
   facilitating learning, 33–34
   goals, 34, 36
   for group membership and leadership
     by laboratory methods, 75–77
   problems of, 36–40
   relearning of attitudes and motives, 35
   sensitivity-training groups, 76
   T-groups, 76n
Trist, E., 30, 50, 52, 90, 92, 97, 101
"Two-step" flow of communications, 93
Typology, of organizations, 44–47, 63

U

Underproducers, 61
Unions, 15, 45, 60, 67, 68, 70, 91:
   labor-management bargaining commit-
     tee, 73
   and psychological contract, 47, 50
   oil-refinery labor-management conflict,
     74–75, 77
Union stewards, 63

V

Validity of the predictor, 21
Variable production, 33
Vertical cliques, 69
Violations of the psychological contract,
   46–47
Vroom, V. H., 61, 62, 64n

W

Wallach, M. A., 79
Wash-out rates, 21–22
Weber, M., 12
Western Electric Co., 27–30
Whyte, W. F., 61
Win-lose situations among groups, 82, 85,
   86
World War II, 21, 53

Z

Zalesnik, A., 61